MERSEY SHIPPING
Remembered

MERSEY SHIPPING
Remembered

Ian Collard

TEMPUS

First published 2003

Tempus Publishing Limited
The Mill, Brimscombe Port,
Stroud, Gloucestershire, GL5 2QG

British Library Cataloguing in Publication Data.
A catalogue record for this book is available from the British Library.

ISBN 0 7524 2815 2

Typesetting and origination by Tempus Publishing Limited
Printed in Great Britain by Midway Colour Print, Wiltshire

Contents

Acknowledgements

I would like to thank Duncan Haws for the wealth of information he has provided; G.H. Elliot of Chr. Salvesen & Co.; *The Journal of Commerce* and The World Ship Society for all the help and assistance given to me in the preparation of this work; and John Luxton and Gary Andrews.

Introduction

Ships have sailed in and out of the Mersey for hundreds of years. From 1715 when the first dock was built, up to the completion of the Royal Seaforth Terminals in 1971, the dock infrastructure has been enlarged, modified and improved.

Most of the development took place in Victorian times when Britain held a major role in shipping, commerce, banking, insurance, engineering and manufacturing. The Mersey Docks & Harbour Board responded to the demands of the economy by modernising the system and creating new docks, locks and warehouses.

One of the port's main advantages was that it was the main gateway for the North Atlantic trade to American and Canadian ports. It was from Liverpool that Samuel Cunard started the first steamship services across the Atlantic in 1840 and many other shipping lines were formed in that period.

The Mersey Docks & Harbour Board was created through an 1857 Act of Parliament that removed all jurisdictions over the dock estate from the Town Council. The Board then purchased land on both sides of the river under the provisions of The General Works Act, 1858, completed improvements to Morpeth Dock, reclaimed land by extending the docks into the river, and built new docks in Birkenhead and Wallasey.

In 1890 work commenced on creating a fourteen-mile channel to the Bar and this was followed by the building of banks and revetments on either side to prevent erosion. This work has enabled large cargo, passenger and oil tankers to enter the port with the expert assistance of experienced river pilots. The river and channel are dredged to maintain a satisfactory depth on a regular basis by the dock company's specialist vessels.

The Gladstone Dock was opened in 1913 and completed in 1927, oil jetties were built in 1960 at Tranmere to allow large tankers to discharge, and in 1962 the new Langton Entrance was opened. The 1970s saw the completion of the Royal Seaforth Terminals that provided shipping operators with the most up-to-date port facilities for dealing with containers, timber and refrigerated cargos.

Mr G.W. Brimyard, Managing Director of the Mersey Docks & Harbour Co. said, in 1972, that the new facility at Seaforth would not be the new Port of Liverpool. He stressed that whilst it was a major new asset and addition to the port, the ability to handle every type of trade over the whole dock area would have to play an equal part in the future prosperity of the port. Although conventional and specialised cargos continue to play a role in the work of the port, the main activity is now carried out at the Royal Seaforth Dock, leaving many of the other docks empty and forlorn.

The port itself extended for seven miles on the Liverpool side of the river and for four miles at Birkenhead. The total port area was nearly 2,500 acres in which there were more than thirty-seven miles of quays, and a greater volume of deep-sea exports were handled at Liverpool than any other British port.

It was the beginning of the container revolution which saw the end of conventional cargo handling and traditional ships. Mersey Docks & Harbour Co. invested in new sheds, quays and facilities for established cargo systems and these were out of date soon after they were commissioned. Vittoria Dock was completely rebuilt for the Far East services of the Blue Funnel Line and a £2 million scheme was completed for Clan Line services to India, Pakistan and South Africa.

The realisation that containerisation was revolutionising the carriage of goods by sea meant that most shipping operators needed to invest in new vessels which were purpose built for this trade. Many of the conventional ships were made redundant and sold to overseas operators for further trading, while some were sold for demolition. Relatively new vessels that had given their owners a small return on their investment were sold and major shipping lines vanished from the maritime scene.

I was fortunate to be there to record theses changes and to witness the end of a chapter in the history of British shipping and the Port of Liverpool. I would travel over to Liverpool on the ferry and spend most weekends photographing the liners, cargo vessels and Irish Sea ferry movements. In the summer, my Isle of Man Steam Packet contract allowed me to travel to Douglas each Saturday and to Llandudno in North Wales on a Sunday, and enabled me to capture photographs of vessels underway in the Channel and anchored at the Bar.

The book is a record of this time of change and upheaval in the life of a maritime centre and one that will be remembered by everyone involved in the shipping and associated industries on Merseyside. The docks are now starting to be developed by housing schemes, new hotels and marinas but the ships shown in this book will never be seen again in the port.

One

The Liners

Ever since Cunard Line's paddle steamer *Britannia* sailed from Liverpool on her maiden voyage in 1840, the Port of Liverpool has provided facilities for passenger liners. Many famous Cunard Line vessels have sailed from Princes Landing Stage on regular transatlantic voyages to North America and Canada, and *Aquitania*, *Lusitania*, *Mauretania*, *Franconia* and *Britannic* all sailed from Liverpool. *Empress of Britain*, *Empress of France*, *Empress of Canada* and their famous fleet-mates provided passenger services from Liverpool to Canadian ports. *Aureol*, *Apapa* and *Accra* linked the port with West Africa, and the Anchor Line vessels *Caledonia*, *Circassia* and *Cilicia* sailed to India and Pakistan.

Bibby, Booth, Blue Star and Blue Funnel Line also provided passenger accommodation on their vessels sailing from Liverpool to India, South America, South Africa and Australia. Although all of these services ceased to operate in the 1970s because of the strong competition from the airlines, some cruise vessels continued to call at the port to provide cruises to the Mediterranean and Atlantic Islands.

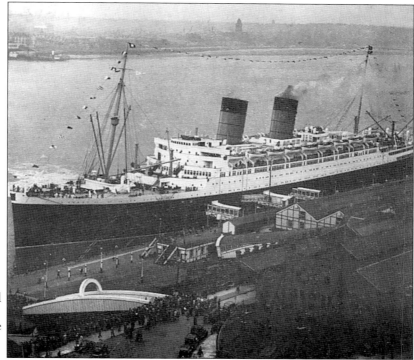

The Cunard liner *Mauretania* sailing from the Liverpool Landing Stage on her maiden voyage to New York on 17 June 1939.

Britannic was built by Harland & Wolff at Belfast. She was launched on 6 August 1929 and sailed on her maiden voyage from Liverpool to New York on 28 June 1930. On 10 May 1934 the Cunard Line and White Star Line amalgamated to become Cunard-White Star Line and *Britannic* made her first voyage from London to New York on 19 April 1935. She was requisitioned by the British government on 29 August 1939 and operated as a troopship, being attacked by enemy aircraft in the Red Sea in October 1940 and by U-boats in the Atlantic. She survived the Second World War and returned to the Liverpool to New York service on 22 May 1948. In June 1950 she collided with the American cargo vessel *Pioneer Land* in New York harbour. Each winter she cruised in the Mediterranean and completed several world cruises with Caronia. She suffered a broken crankshaft in 1960 and was laid-up briefly at New York. On 25 November 1960 she sailed on her last voyage from New York to Liverpool as the last vessel to sail the North Atlantic in the colours of the White Star Line. *Britannic* was sold to the shipbreakers at Inverkeithing and sailed from Liverpool on 16 December 1960 to be broken up by T.W. Ward.

Ivernia was launched on 14 December 1954 at John Brown's Shipyard at Clydeside. She sailed on her maiden voyage from Greenock to Montreal on 1 July 1955 and from Liverpool to Montreal on 27 July 1955. In 1962 she was re-fitted by John Brown on the Clyde and was renamed *Franconia*, with accommodation for 119 first class and 728 tourist class passengers. Before being transferred to the New York to Bermuda service in 1967, her tonnage was increased to 22,637 and she was painted white. *Franconia* was laid up in December 1971 and, in 1973, she was sold to the Black Sea Steamship Co. to sail under the Soviet flag. Renamed *Fedor Shalyapin*, she sailed on her first voyage from Southampton to Sydney and Auckland on 20 November 1973.

Carinthia was the third sister in the Saxonia class to enter service. She was built on the Clyde by John Brown and sailed on her maiden voyage from Liverpool to New York on 27 June 1956. She sailed from Liverpool to New York in the winter months. In 1967 *Carinthia* was repainted white for cruising and, after making her last passenger sailing for the Cunard Line in October that year, was laid up at Southampton. In May 1968 she was sold to the Sitmar Line and was initially renamed *Fairland* for the line's Southampton to New Zealand service, continuing to lay-up at Southampton. Sitmar Line completed a restyling of the vessel at a yard in Trieste in 1970-1971 and she entered service in the American cruise market in 1972 as *Fairsea*. She was able to accommodate 910 first class passengers and her tonnage was increased to 21,916 tons. When P&O purchased the Sitmar Line in 1988 she was renamed *Fair Princess* and, in 2000, became *China Seas Discovery* owned by Emerald Cruises. She was laid up at Kaohsiung in 2002 and it was announced that in 2003 she would be based at Keelung, providing one-night gambling trips for four nights a week and also three-night cruises to Naha and Ishigaki in Japan.

Saxonia was launched by Lady Churchill at John Brown's Shipyard at Glasgow on 17 February 1954 and sailed on her maiden voyage from Liverpool to Montreal on 2 September of that year. She was the first of four sisters built for the Cunard Line service to Quebec and Montreal. In 1961 she was employed on the London to New York service and cruised out of Port Everglades in the winter months. She was sent back to her builders in 1962 to be converted to a dual-purpose North Atlantic and cruise liner, painted Caronia green and renamed *Carmania*. Between 1964 and 1970 she was employed on 'fly-cruises' in the Mediterranean during the summer and Caribbean cruises in the winter, being painted white in 1967. *Carmania* was laid up at Southampton in 1971 and was moored in the River Fal in 1972. She was sold to Nikreis Maritime Corporation in 1973 and renamed *Leonid Sobinov*, managed by CTC Lines for both the Southampton to Australia and New Zealand service and cruising. As *Leonid Sobinov* she operated a variety of services and cruises until 1999 when she was delivered to Indian shipbreakers at Alang on 1 October that year. She had, since 1 April, been anchored off Alang.

Media was the first new vessel built for the Cunard Line following the Second World War. She sailed on her maiden voyage from Liverpool to New York on 20 August 1947. In 1952 she was fitted with stabilizers and her promenade deck was glazed. *Media* and her sister ship *Parthia* were dual cargo-passenger vessels and it eventually became uneconomical to operate them. *Media's* last passenger sailing for the Cunard Line was in September 1961 from Liverpool to Quebec and Montreal. She was sold to Cogeder Line, Genoa, in 1961 and was modernised and rebuilt by Officine A&R Navi at Genoa where, renamed *Flavia*, she was able to accommodate 1,224 passengers in one class. *Flavia* was initially employed on the Genoa to Australia route and, later, the Bremerhaven, Southampton to Australia route. In 1968 she was cruising in the Mediterranean with winter cruises in the Caribbean. She was sold to Costa Armatori S.p.A of Naples in 1969 and cruised out of Miami. She was sold to Flavian Shipping S.A. Panama, renamed *Flavian* and laid up at Hong Kong in 1982. In 1986 she was purchased by Lavia Shipping of Panama, renamed *Lavia* and again laid up at Hong Kong. On 7 January 1989 she suffered a serious fire, was beached and declared a total loss.

Fairstar was built as *Oxfordshire* for the Bibby Line and operated as a troopship. She was delivered by Fairfield on 13 February 1957 and, up to 1962, she sailed as Britain's last troop carrier. Following her final trooping voyage from Southampton to Malta in 1962 she was laid up in the River Fal. The following year she was chartered for six years to the Fairline Shipping Corporation and was converted to a passenger liner at Schiedam. In 1964 she was purchased by the Sitmar Line and renamed *Fairstar*. On 19 May of that year she sailed from Southampton to Brisbane and, in 1973, she was converted for cruising out of Australia. In 1988 the Sitmar Line was taken over by P&O Lines and in 1991 *Fairstar* was transferred to the Fairstar Shipping Corporation. Renamed *Ripa*, she was broken up at Alang in 1997.

Arkadia, built as *Monarch of Bermuda*, was owned by Furness Withy and operated on their New York to Hamilton, Bermuda service. She and her sister, *Queen of Bermuda*, left New York at 15.00 on Saturdays, arriving at St Georges, Bermuda at 09.00 on Mondays where passengers were tendered to Hamilton. They departed on Wednesday, arriving at New York at 08.00 on the Friday. In 1939 *Arkadia* became a troop carrier and operated to Norway, Italy, Portugal and North Africa; at the end of hostilities she had transported 164,840 personnel and steamed 450,512 miles. On 24 March 1947, whilst being converted back to a passenger vessel, she was almost destroyed by fire. The Ministry of Transport purchased her and, after her rebuild by J.I. Thornycroft, she was renamed *New Australia* and worked as an emigrant carrier. She sailed on her first voyage from Southampton to Sydney on 15 August 1950, managed by Shaw, Savill & Albion. In 1953 she carried troops to Korea and, in 1958, was sold to the Greek Line and refitted by Bloom & Voss at Hamburg, being renamed *Arkadia*. Following this refit she was able to carry 150 first class and 1,150 tourist class passengers. She sailed on her first voyage for the line from Bremerhaven to Quebec and Montreal on 22 May 1958. Her passenger accommodation was altered again by Bloom & Voss in 1961. She was finally sold to shipbreakers at Valencia, where she arrived on 18 December 1966.

North Atlantic routes and mileages by Canadian Pacific 'Empress' liners.

Canadian Pacific — **BAR PRICE LIST**

	Per Glass s. d.
WHISKY—SCOTCH	
White Heather, Black Label, Haig's " Dimple "	1 9
Other Proprietary Brands	1 6
IRISH	
Jameson's	1 6
CANADIAN & AMERICAN	
Old Grandad	1 9
Other Proprietary Brands	1 6
GIN	
Proprietary Brands	1 6
VODKA	
Proprietary Brands	1 6
RUM	
Bacardi, Carta de Oro, Carta Blanca	1 9
Other Proprietary Brands	1 6
BRANDY	
Proprietary XXX Brands	2 0
BRANDY—LIQUEUR	
Hennessey XO	3 3
Hine Grande Champagne	3 0
Cordon Bleu	2 9
Bisquit Dubouché V.S.O.P.	2 6
Courvoisier V.S.O.P.	2 6
	Glass s. d.
LIQUEURS	
Chartreuse, Yellow or Green, Cointreau, Grand Marnier	
Advocaat, Apricot Brandy, Benedictine, Drambuie, Glayva Scotch, Kummel — ALL	2 0
Cherry Heering, Crème de Menthe, Curaçao, Tia Maria, Van der Hum Cherry Brandy, Crème de Cacao	
COCKTAILS	
MIXED TO ORDER	from 2/- to 6 /-
PORT	
Sandemans, Double Diamond, Royal Dry	1 9
Rover Rich, Very Fine Tawny	1 6
Australian Fine Ruby	1 0

	Per Glass s. d.
SHERRY	
Bristol Cream	2 6
Bristol Dry, Bristol Milk	2 3
Tio Pepe, Jerez Cream, Dry Sack	2 0
Dry Fly, Fleet	1 9
South African, Sweet, Pale Dry	1 0
MIXED and FANCY DRINKS	
Planters Punch	2 6
John Collins, Tom Collins, Gin Rickey	2 6
Pimms No. 1	2 6
FIZZES Gin, Silver, Golden	2 9
FLIPS or NOGS Brandy	3 0
Port, Sherry	2 6
Gin, Whisky, Rum	2 6
SOURS Rye	2 3
Whisky, Gin, Rum	2 3
ALES and STOUTS	Per Bottle s. d.
Bass, Worthington, Guinness, Strong Scotch Ale Nips	1 4
CANADIAN	
Dow, Molson, Carling, O'Keefe, Labatt	1 4
LAGERS	Per Bottle
Danish, English	1 6
Canadian	1 4
LAGERS—DRAUGHT	Imp. ½ pt.
Danish	10
English	9
MINERAL WATERS	Bot. s. d. / Split s. d.
Ginger Ale (Canada Dry)	1 2 / 8
Ginger Ale, Soda, Tonic Water, Lemonade	9 / 6
Grape Fruit, Ginger Beer	9
Bitter Lemon, Bitter Orange	8 / 6
Coca Cola	8
Seven Up	7

	Glass Plain s. d.	with Soda s. d.
CORDIALS and SQUASHES		
Lime Juice, Lemon Squash, Orange Squash	4	10
Fresh Fruit Squash	6	1 0
CIDER		½ pt. Bot.
Bulmer, Gaymer		1 0
Babycham		Bot. 1 3
CIGARETTES (Virginia)	20 s Pkt. s. d.	
Sobranie, Cocktail	3 0	
Super Virginia, State Express 555, Players No. 3, Special Filter B & H	2 0	
Churchman No. 1, Piccadilly No. 1, Senior Service, Capstan, Players, Gold Leaf Filter, Craven ' A ' Cork Tip, Craven ' A ' F.T., Du Maurier F.T., Rothmans F.T., State Express F.T., Piccadilly F.T.	1 9	
CANADIAN		
Sweet Caporal, McDonald Export, Players Mild, Matinee, Viceroy, Mayfair, Cameo Menthol	1 9	
AMERICAN		
Phillip Morris, Pall Mall, Marlboro' Camel, Lucky Strike, Chesterfield	1 9	
TURKISH		
Balkan Sobranie	25's Pkt. 4 2	
Abdulla No. 11	10's Pkt. 1 3	
RUSSIAN		
Sobranie Black	25's Pkt. 3 2	
CIGARS		
Havana	from 1/- to 3 9 each	
Jamaican	2/3 & 2/9	
British	from 9d. to 1/6 each	
TOBACCO		
Balkan Sobranie Mixture, Three Nuns, Players No Name 5/- for 2 oz.		
John Cotton Nos. 1 & 2	4/6	
Capstan Full and Medium, Gold Block.	4 -	
Craven Mixture	3/9	
Four Square (Red) St. Bruno Flake	3/6	
Imperial Mixture	2/9	
Irish Cake	2/0	

Full details of Wines, Spirits etc. are shown in Comprehensive Wine List, available on request from Head Waiters, Wine Stewards and Barkeepers   PRINTED IN ENGLAND

Empress of Scotland was launched as *Empress of Japan* for the Canadian Pacific Vancouver to Yokohama service by Fairfield at Glasgow. She took her maiden voyage from Liverpool to Quebec on 14 June 1930, returning to Southampton where she sailed on 12 July to Suez, Hong Kong, Yokohama and Vancouver. In 1939 she was requisitioned as a troop carrier and, in 1942, she was renamed *Empress of Scotland*. Released from war duties on 3 May 1948 she was refitted at Glasgow and Liverpool, and sailed on her first post-war voyage from Liverpool to Quebec on 9 May 1950. Her masts were shortened in 1952 to allow her to pass under the Quebec Bridge and sail to Montreal. In 1958 she was sold to the Hamburg-Atlantic Line, renamed *Hanseatic*, and sent to be refitted and modernised by Howaldt at Hamburg. On 19 July 1958 she sailed from Hamburg, Havre and Southampton to New York and operated cruises during the winter months. After being badly damaged, having caught fire at New York on 7 September 1966, *Hanseatic* was towed to Hamburg where she was sold for scrap and broken up by Eisen & Metall AG.

38-day West Indies and Rio Cruise

Sailing from Liverpool 8th Jan. 1968

Fares from £355 (Shore Excursions not included)

PORT	ARRIVE		DEPART	MILES
Liverpool		·--	8 Mon. 5 pm	1650
Las Palmas	Jan. 12 Fri. 10 a.m.		12 Fri. Midnight	2815
Trinidad	Jan. 19 Fri. 7 a.m.		20 Sat. 1 a.m.	97
Grenada	Jan. 20 Sat. 8 a.m.		Jan. 20 Sat. 9 p.m.	150
Barbados	Jan. 21 Sun. 8 a.m.		Jan. 22 Mon. 2 p.m.	3081
Rio de Janeiro	Jan. 29 Mon. 2 p.m.		Jan. 31 Wed. 8 p.m.	2761
Dakar	Feb. 6 Tue. Midnight		Feb. 7 Wed. Midnight	880
Teneriffe	Feb. 10 Sat. 8 a.m.		Feb. 10 Sat. 4 p.m.	270
Madeira	Feb. 11 Sun. 8 a.m.		Feb. 11 Sun. p.m.	1428
Liverpool	Feb. 15 Thur. 8 a.m.			13132

ROOM NUMBERS

LINE	DECK			ROOM NUMBERS
1	A DECK	Outside	1 Bed, Bath and Toilet	A.130
2		Inside	1 Bed, Bath and Toilet	A.39, A.40, A.41, A.42, A.58, A.65, A.66, A.87,
3		Outside	1 Bed, Shower and Toilet	A.3, A.6, A.9, A.12,
4		Inside	1 Bed, Shower and Toilet	A.69, A.71, A.75, A.77, A.114, A.120.
5		Inside	1 Bed, Shower and Toilet	A.37, A.38, A.68, A.70.
5		Inside	1 Bed, Shower and Toilet	A.5, A.7, A.8, A.10, A.134, A.135, A.139,
6		Outside	2 Beds, Bath and Toilet	A.45, A.46, A.49, A.50, A.89, A.91, A.94, A.97,
7		Outside	2 Beds, Shower and Toilet	A.47, A.48, A.61, A.62.
8		Outside	2 Beds, Shower and Toilet	A.74, A.76, A.115, A.117.
9		Outside	2 Beds, Shower and Toilet	A.15, A.16, A.21, A.22, A.140, A.142, A.147.
10		Inside	2 Beds, Bath and Toilet	A.80, A.86, A.92, A.95.
11		Inside	2 Beds, Shower and Toilet	A.81, A.83, A.122. (See
12		Inside	2 Beds, Shower and Toilet	A.1, A.2, A.4, A.11, Note 4.)
13		Verandah Suites	2 Beds, Bath and Toilet, Sitting Room with Convertible Sofa Bed	A.33, A.34, A.35, A.36,
		Suites	Bedroom, Bathroom, Toilet, Sitting Room	A.45-A.47*, A.46-A.48* A.61*-A.63, A.62*-A.64
14	B DECK	Outside	1 Bed, Shower and Toilet	B.102, B.104, B.112, (See Note 1)
15		Outside	1 Bed, Toilet	B.150, B.151. (See Note1).
16		Inside	1 Bed, Shower and Toilet	B.118, B.140, B.141.
17		Outside	2 Beds, Shower and Toilet	B.165, B.177, B.185.
18		Outside	2 Beds, Toilet	B.100 (See Note 4).
19		Inside	2 Beds, Shower and Toilet	B.173 (See Note 4).
20		Outside	1 Bed	B.1, B.2, B.25, B.27, B.199, B.205, B.209.
21		Inside	1 Bed	B.5, B.6, B.7, B.8, B.14, B.49, B.51, B.52, B.54, B.79, B.80, B.81, B.82, B.110, B.114, B.120, B.133, B.134, B.135, B.158, B.159, B.160,
22		Outside	2 Beds	B.3, B.4, B.9, B.10, B.11, B.37, B.38, B.41, B.42, B.86, B.89, B.92, B.95.
23		Inside	2 Beds	B.24, B.26, B.34, B.39, B.105, B.107, B.108, B.189. B.191. B.195.
24	C DECK	Outside	2 Beds	C.11, C.12, C.16, C.17, C.40, C.42, C.44, C.45, C.63. (See Note 4).
25		Outside	1 Bed, 1 Upper Berth	C.3, C.4, C.7, C.8, C.31,
26		Inside	2 Beds	C.9, C.10, C.14, C.15, C.60, C.61. (See Note 4)
27		Inside	1 Bed, 1 Upper Berth	C.1, C.2, C.5, C.6, C.33,

NOTES:

1. Upper berth may be fitted in these rooms if desired.
2. For day use these four rooms are each fitted with one folding bed and one bed convertible to a sofa
3. Rooms A.83 and A.122 are each fitted with an additional folding upper berth, minimum fare will apply for the third passenger.
4. Upper berths may be fitted in these rooms for third and fourth passengers if desired, minimum fare will apply for extra passengers.

Details of a thirty-eight-day West Indies and Rio cruise by the Canadian Pacific liner *Empress of England*, sailing from Liverpool on 8 January 1968.

Empress of France was launched as *Duchess of Bedford* by John Brown's on the Clyde on 24 January 1928 by Mrs Baldwin, wife of the British Prime Minister. Her maiden voyage from Liverpool to Quebec occurred on 1 June that year. In 1939 she was taken over as a troop carrier and sailed on 29 August from Liverpool to Bombay. She was returned to Canadian Pacific in 1947 and arrived at Govan on 3 March that year to be converted back to a luxury passenger liner. It was initially planned to rename her *Empress of India* but she emerged as *Empress of France*, sailing on her first post-war voyage from Liverpool to Quebec and Montreal on 1 September 1948. *Empress of France* was fitted with new streamlined funnels in the winter of 1958-1959 and, after being sold to the British Iron & Steel Corporation at Newport in 1960, was broken up by J. Cashmore.

An early morning view of *Dunera* (1937/12,620grt) and *Carinthia* (1956/21,947grt) anchored in the River Mersey with *Empress of Britain* (1956/25,516grt) unloading passengers at Princes Landing Stage.

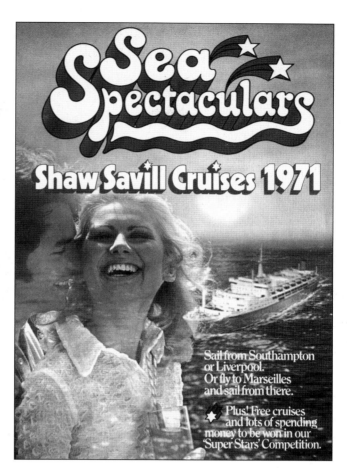

Shaw Savill's 'Sea Spectaculars' 1971 cruise leaflet featuring cruises from Southampton and Liverpool by *Southern Cross*.

Left: Uganda was also built by Barclay, Curle for the British India Line's service from London to East Africa. She sailed on her maiden voyage on 2 August 1951 from London to Beira and was painted with an all-white hull in 1955. The East African service was withdrawn in 1966 and in 1967 *Uganda* was also converted to an educational cruise ship at Howaldswerke in Hamburg. She sailed on her first cruise on 27 February 1968 and in 1972 ownership was transferred to the P&O Line. She was taken over by the British government on 10 April 1982 and used as a hospital ship in the Falkland Islands. She resumed cruises briefly later that year but was chartered to the government again in 1983 for use between the Ascension Islands and the Falklands. She returned to the UK in 1985 and in 1986 was laid up and sold to An Hsiung Iron & Steel Co., shipbreakers, being renamed *Triton* for the delivery voyage to Kaohsiung, where she arrived on 15 July. She had been registered in the ownership of Triton Shipping Co., Barbados for the voyage to the breakers, and was anchored outside the harbour while negotiations took place as to a possible re-sale. On 22 August, however, she was driven aground by typhoon Wayne and heeled over onto her side, being demolished as she lay.

Opposite: Nevasa, British India Line, 1956, 20,746grt, 186m x 24m, 17 knots. *Nevasa* was built by Barclay, Curle as a troop transport and was delivered to the British India Line on 12 July 1956. When the troop service ended in 1962 she was laid up in the River Fal. She was rebuilt in 1964/65 for use as an educational cruise ship, with accommodation for 307 passengers in cabins and 783 children in dormitories. The British India Line was taken over by the P&O Group in 1972 and *Nevasa* was broken up at Kaoshiung in 1975.

BRITISH INDIA   Summary of Cruises 1970

Ship	No.	Days	Date	Itinerary	Fare
NEVASA	168	20	3 Feb.	Southampton, Le Havre, Teneriffe, Freetown, Dakar, Casablanca, Le Havre, Southampton.	£150—£200
UGANDA	175	16	13 Feb.	Southampton, Tangier, Malta G.C., Haifa (Jerusalem), Rhodes (Lindos), Corfu, Venice, U.K. (Gatwick) by air.	£125—£175
NEVASA	170	15	24 Feb.	Southampton, Malaga (Granada), Piraeus (Athens), Istanbul, Itea (Delphi), Venice, U.K. (Gatwick) by air.	£125—£175
UGANDA	177	15	1/2 Mar.	U.K. (Gatwick) by air, Venice, Piraeus (Athens), Alexandria (Cairo), Malta G.C., Gibraltar, Liverpool.	£125—£175
NEVASA	172	14	11/12 Mar.	U.K. (Gatwick) by air, Venice, Santorin, Izmir (Ephesus), Alexandria (Cairo), Haifa (Jerusalem), Itea (Delphi), Rijeka, U.K. (Gatwick) by air.	£135—£185
UGANDA	179	14	18 Mar.	Liverpool, Malaga, Palma, Oran, Lisbon. Liverpool.	£120—£170
NEVASA	174	16	25/26 Mar.	U.K. (Gatwick) by air, Rijeka, Santorin, Istanbul, Itea (Delphi), Syracuse, Tangier, Liverpool. I.A.P.S. CHARTER CRUISE	I.A.P.S.
UGANDA	181	14	3 Apl.	Southampton, Gibraltar, Tangier, Madeira. Lisbon, Southampton.	£112—£162
NEVASA	176	14	12 Apl.	Liverpool, Madeira, Oran, Cadiz, Lisbon, Liverpool.	£112—£162
UGANDA	183	14	20 Apl.	Leith, Vigo, Tangier, Gibraltar, Lisbon, Zeebrugge (Bruges), Leith.	£112—£162
NEVASA	178	10	28 Apl.	Southampton, Vigo, Gibraltar, Tangier, Lisbon, Southampton.	£ 82—£132
UGANDA	185	11	6 May.	Leith, Corunna, Lisbon, Cherbourg, Zeebrugge (Bruges), Leith.	£ 88—£138
NEVASA	180	10	9 May	Tilbury, Gothenburg, Copenhagen, Bergen, Tilbury.	£ 82—£127
UGANDA	187	14	19 May	Leith, Vigo, Gibraltar, Malaga, Lisbon, Clyde. AYRSHIRE CHARTER CRUISE	
NEVASA	182	11	20 May	Tilbury, Corunna, Gibraltar, Ceuta (Tetuan), Lisbon, Tilbury.	£ 92—£142
UGANDA	189	14	3 June	Clyde, Madeira, Teneriffe, Casablanca, Lisbon, Clyde.	£120—£170
NEVASA	184	14	4 June	Leith, Stockholm, Helsinki, Leningrad (Moscow), Copenhagen, Leith.	£120—£170
UGANDA	191	14	19 June	Clyde, Ponta Delgada (Azores), Madeira, Ceuta (Tetuan), Lisbon, Clyde. GLASGOW CHARTER CRUISE	£120—£170
NEVASA	186	15	20 June	Sunderland, Teneriffe, Madeira, Casablanca, Lisbon, Sunderland.	£125—£175
UGANDA	193	14	5 July	Swansea, Madeira, Teneriffe, Lanzarote, Tangier, Swansea.	£127—£177
NEVASA	188	14	7 July	Leith, Visby (Gotland), Leningrad (Moscow), Copenhagen, Oslo, Leith.	£127—£177
UGANDA	195	15	21 July	Southampton, Copenhagen, Leningrad (Moscow), Stockholm, Kristiansand, Southampton.	£138—£188
NEVASA	190	15	24 July	Southampton, Lagos (Portugal), Alghero (Sardinia), Balearic Isles, Algiers, Malaga, Gibraltar, Southampton.	£140—£190
UGANDA	197	14	6 Aug	Southampton, Ponta Delgada (Azores), Madeira, Teneriffe, Casablanca, Southampton.	£135—£185
NEVASA	192	16	10 Aug.	Southampton, Ceuta (Tetuan), Mahon (Minorca), Cagliari (Sardinia), Elba, Leghorn (Pisa and Florence), Gibraltar, Southampton.	£152—£202
UGANDA	199	14	21 Aug.	Southampton, Ceuta (Tetuan), Ibiza, Tarragona, Malaga, Gibraltar, Southampton.	£135—£185
NEVASA	194	13	28 Aug.	Liverpool, Madeira, Teneriffe, Las Palmas, Vigo, Liverpool. H.A.S.S.R.A. CHARTER CRUISE*	
UGANDA	201	7	6 Sept.	Details to be arranged later. NATIONAL TRUST FOR SCOTLAND CRUISE*	
NEVASA	196	13	11 Sept.	Liverpool, Madeira, Teneriffe, Las Palmas, Vigo, Liverpool. H.A.S.S.R.A. CHARTER CRUISE*	
UGANDA	203	21	14 Sept.	Dublin, Malta G. C., Venice, Rhodes, Tangier, Dublin. AUGUSTINIAN CHARTER CRUISE*	
NEVASA	198	14	27 Sept.	Liverpool, Casablanca, Teneriffe, Madeira, Lisbon, Liverpool.	£120—£170
UGANDA	205	15	10 Oct.	Southampton, Gibraltar, Malta G.C., Heraklion (Knossos), Istanbul, Piraeus (Athens), Venice, U.K. (Gatwick) by air.	£140—£190
NEVASA	200	14	13 Oct.	Liverpool, Gibraltar, Leghorn (Pisa and Florence), Ajaccio (Corsica), Lisbon, Liverpool.	£120—£170
UGANDA	207	13	25/26 Oct.	U.K. (Gatwick) by air, Venice, Tripoli (North Africa), Piraeus (Athens), Izmir (Ephesus), Corfu, Rijeka, U.K. (Gatwick) by air.	£135—£185
NEVASA	202	15	29 Oct.	Southampton, Lisbon, Naples, Capri, Delos/Mykonos, Izmir (Ephesus), Venice, U.K. (Gatwick) by air.	£140—£190
UGANDA	209	13	7/8 Nov.	U.K. (Gatwick) by air, Rijeka, Nauplia (Epidaurus, Mycenae and old Corinth), Piraeus (Athens), Beirut (Baalbek), Famagusta, Venice, U.K. (Gatwick) by air.	£130—£180
NEVASA	204	15	13/14 Nov.	U.K. (Gatwick) by air, Venice, Piraeus (Athens), Alexandria (Cairo), Malta G.C., Lisbon, Southampton.	£130—£180

British India Line's Summary of Cruises, 1970.

Ceramic, Shaw Savill Line, 1948, 15,896grt, 171m x 22m, 17 knots. She was sold and broken up in 1972.

Monte Umbe, Naviera Aznar S.A., 1959, 9,971grt, 155m x 19m, 16½ knots. She was renamed *Liban* in 1975 and broken up in Pakistan in 1979.

Monte Ulia, Naviera Aznar S.A., 1952, 10,123grt, 148m x 19m, 16½ knots. She was built as *Monasterio de El Escorial* and became *Monte Ulia* in 1952. On 13 October 1975, while undergoing repairs at the Sestao yard at Bilbao, she sustained considerable damage when a fire broke out.

Opposite: Cilicia, Anchor Line, 1938, 11,137grt, 154m x 20m, 18 knots. *Cilicia* was built by Fairfield's at Glasgow and was launched on 21 October 1937, entering service on Anchor Line's Liverpool to Bombay route in 1938. She became an armed merchant cruiser in 1939 and also operated as a troop transport during the Second World War. Her first post-war voyage took place on 31 May 1947 when she left Liverpool for Bombay. In 1965, when Anchor Line closed the passenger service, *Cilicia* and her sisters *Caledonia* and *Circassia* were advertised for sale. *Cilicia* was sold in November 1965 to Stichting Vakopleiding Havenbedrief, Rotterdam, and was converted to a training vessel, being renamed *Jan Backx*. She was sold to shipbreakers in Spain in 1980.

Monte Anaga, Naviera Aznar S.A., 1959, 6,813grt, 150m x 18m, 16 knots. In 1975 she was sold to the Government of Mexico to be used as a training ship and was renamed *Primero De Junio*.

APPROXIMATE SAILING & ARRIVAL DATES MAY 70-AP 71

LIVERPOOL-CANARY ISLANDS

	VOY. NO.	LEAVE LIVERPOOL	VIGO	ARRIVE CANARIES	LEAVE CANARIES	VIGO	DUE LIVERPOOL
MONTE ANAGA	16	5 May		11 May	12 May	15 May	18 May
MONTE UMBE		13 May		CRUISE 1 "WINE CRUISE"			28 May
MONTE ANAGA	17	19 May	22 May	25 May	26 May	29 May	1 June
MONTE UMBE		29 May		CRUISE 2 "ATLANTIC CRUISE"			13 June
MONTE ANAGA	18	1 June		MINI-CRUISE TO LISBON AND VIGO			9 June
MONTE ANAGA	19	9 June	12 June	15 June	16 June	19 June	22 June
MONTE UMBE		13 June		CRUISE 3 "MEDITERRANEAN CRUISE"			28 June
MONTE ANAGA	20	23 June	26 June	29 June	30 June	3 July	6 July
MONTE ANAGA	21	7 July	10 July	13 July	14 July	17 July	20 July
MONTE ANAGA	22	21 July	24 July	27 July	28 July	31 July	3 Aug.
MONTE ANAGA	23	4 Aug.	7 Aug.	10 Aug.	11 Aug.	14 Aug.	17 Aug.
MONTE ANAGA	24	18 Aug.	21 Aug.	24 Aug.	25 Aug.	28 Aug.	31 Aug.
MONTE ANAGA	25	1 Sept.	4 Sept.	7 Sept.	8 Sept.	11 Sept.	14 Sept.
MONTE ANAGA	26	15 Sept.	18 Sept.	21 Sept.	22 Sept.	25 Sept.	To Bilbao
MONTE UMBE		28 Sept.		CRUISE 4 "SUMMER CRUISE"			12 Oct.
MONTE UMBE		13 Oct.		CRUISE 5 "AUTUMN CRUISE"			27 Oct.
MONTE ANAGA	1	19 Oct.		25 Oct.	26 Oct.		1 Nov.
MONTE ANAGA	2	2 Nov.		8 Nov.	9 Nov.		15 Nov.
MONTE ANAGA	3	16 Nov.		22 Nov.	23 Nov.		29 Nov.
MONTE ANAGA	4	30 Nov.		6 Dec.	7 Dec.		13 Dec.
MONTE URQUIOLA				13 Dec. (Tfe)	14 Dec. (L.P.)		20 Dec.
MONTE ANAGA	5	14 Dec.		20 Dec.	21 Dec.		27 Dec.
MONTE URQUIOLA	1	21 Dec.	24 Dec.	27 Dec.	28 Dec.		3 Jan. 71
MONTE ANAGA	6	28 Dec.		3 Jan. 71	4 Jan.		10 Jan.
MONTE URQUIOLA	2	4 Jan. 71	7 Jan.	10 Jan.	11 Jan.		17 Jan.
MONTE ANAGA	7	11 Jan.		17 Jan.	18 Jan.		24 Jan.
MONTE URQUIOLA	3	18 Jan.	21 Jan.	24 Jan.	25 Jan.		31 Jan.
MONTE ANAGA	8	25 Jan.		31 Jan.	1 Feb.		7 Feb.
MONTE URQUIOLA	4	1 Feb.	4 Feb.	7 Feb.	8 Feb.		14 Feb.
MONTE ANAGA	9	8 Feb.		14 Feb.	15 Feb.		21 Feb.
MONTE URQUIOLA	5	15 Feb.	18 Feb.	21 Feb.	22 Feb.		28 Feb.
MONTE ANAGA	10	22 Feb.		28 Feb.	1 Mar.		7 Mar.
MONTE URQUIOLA	6	1 Mar.	4 Mar.	7 Mar.	8 Mar.		14 Mar.
MONTE ANAGA	11	8 Mar.		14 Mar.	15 Mar.		21 Mar.
MONTE URQUIOLA	7	15 Mar.	18 Mar.	21 Mar.	22 Mar.		28 Mar.
MONTE ANAGA	12	22 Mar.		28 Mar.	29 Mar.		4 Apl.
MONTE URQUIOLA	8	29 Mar.	1 Apl.	4 Apl.	5 Apl.		11 Apl.
MONTE ANAGA	13	5 Apr.		11 Apl.	12 Apl.		18 Apl.
MONTE URQUIOLA	9	12 Apr.	15 Apl.	18 Apl.	19 Apl.		25 Apl.
MONTE ANAGA	14	19 Apr.		25 Apl.	26 Apl.		2 May
MONTE URQUIOLA	10	26 Apl.	29 Apl.	2 May	TO BILBAO		

Monte Granada, Naviera Aznar S.A., 1975, 10,829grt, 151m x 21m, 22 knots. *Monte Granada* was built by Union Naval de Levente, Valencia, and sailed on her maiden voyage from Liverpool to the Canary Islands on 7 October 1975. She operated from Amsterdam and Southampton to Santander during the winter months. Her sister *Monte Toledo* (1974/10,851grt) commenced her maiden voyage to the Canary Islands from London's Millwall Docks on 12 March 1974. Both vessels were designed with a dual role of a passenger/car ferry, carrying 798 passengers and 300 cars. In winter they were employed on cruises to the Canary Islands, with a capacity for 388 passengers. All passenger and cargo services provided by Anznar between British ports and Spain were terminated in 1977, and *Monte Granada* and *Monte Toledo* were sold to Libyan buyers. Owned by Libya's Ministry of Maritime Transport, *Monte Granada* became *Garnata* and *Monte Toledo* was renamed *Toletela*. Both vessels were laid up early in 2003.

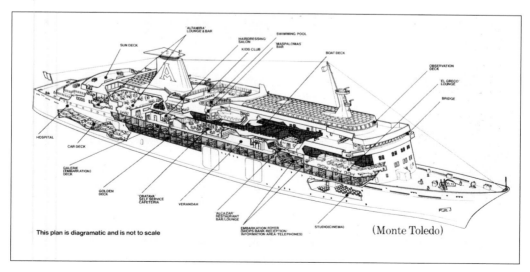

(Monte Toledo)

Alhambra – Granada, Spain

Costa de Lisboa – Cascais, Lisb[on]

Azerbaydzhan AZ62

Liverpool for the Med

14 nights cruise from £818
29 September-13 October '93

Another escape to sunshine from Liverpool, this time to relaxing sunny days in the Western Mediterranean. Start with a good long visit to Lisbon to explore the sights of the city, the nearby resorts of Estoril and Cascais or the woodland paradise of Sintra. Then do the resorts of the Costa del Sol or Andalusia's marvellous Moorish cities, Granada and Cordoba. Follow that with a fun day in Majorca and another day divided between crawling over the Rock of British Gib and beetling through the bazaars of Tangier. Take a couple of days at sea to relax and enjoy a final fling in Dublin.

LIVERPOOL
Wed 29 Sep. Sails 1700 hrs

LISBON (Portugal)
Stay 18 hrs. Sat 2 Oct.
Arr 0800 Dep Sun 3 Oct 0200 hrs
Have your camera ready as the *Azerbaydzhan* sails up the Tagus, under the massive suspension bridge and into Lisbon; it's one of the loveliest sights in the world. But then this is a beautiful city, nestling upon the slopes of seven hills which surround the river so that every turn in the road reveals some astonishing new vista.
Tours: City Sightseeing; Queluz, Sintra & Cascais

MALAGA for Granada (Spain)
Stay 15 hrs. Mon 4 Oct.
Arr 0800 Dep 2300 hrs
When the Moors ruled Spain, Granada was the city they loved best, where they built the palace which is one of the loveliest buildings in the world. The ochre walls of the Alhambra on a hilltop overlooking the city enclose a wonderland of peaceful courtyards and gardens, fountains and pools, and exquisitely beautiful rooms. Don't miss the white Generalife on a nearby hill, or the massive cathedral with its monument to Christopher Columbus.
Tours: Mijas; Granada; Marbella and Puerto Banus

Majorcan Windmills

PALMA (Majorca)
Stay 18 hrs. Wed 6 Oct.
Arr 0800 Dep Thu 7 Oct 0200 hrs
Majorca is one of the Mediterranean's most popular tourist destinations and this is a wonderful opportunity to bask on glorious beaches. But venture inland and you will find that Majorca is also a very pretty island, whether you travel to Valldemosa where Chopin stayed with Georges Sand, or Manacor which is the island's pearl centre, or explore the fabulous subterranean lake in the awesome Caves of Drach.
Tours: City Sightseeing; Manacor & Caves of Drach; Valldemosa

GIBRALTAR
Stay 4½ hrs. Fri 8 Oct.
Arr 0800 Dep 1230 hrs
This little bit of Britain at the gateway to the Mediterranean has red telephone boxes and policemen on the beat. You can go underground to see the wartime headquarters, or up to the peak to see the Barbary Apes, or just enjoy the duty-free shopping Main Street.
Tour: Around the Rock

TANGIER (Morocco)
Stay 6 hrs. Fri 8 Oct
Arr 1500 Dep 2100 hrs
This strategic port has been the setting for all manner of intrigue and adventure throughout its history, and the influence is still there today. As you wander around the kasbah, visit the Dar Shorfa Palace, or explore the Caves of Hercules.
Tour: Tangier & Surroundings

Moroccan Baza[ar]

DUBLIN (Eire)
Stay 13 hrs. Tue 12 Oct.
Arr 0800 Dep 2100 hrs
Just walk beside the Liffey or v[isit] St Patrick's Cathedral, go shop[ping] on Grafton Street or call in at a[ny of] the city's famous pubs, and you'[ll be] able to see for yourself why Dub[lin] has such a marvellous reputati[on] for friendliness and hospitality.
Tours: City Sightseeing; Powersc[ourt] & Glendalough; North Dublin Co[ast] and Malahide

LIVERPOOL
Wed 13 Oct Arr 0800 hrs

Azerbaydzhan AZ 62
Fares in £ Sterling per adult
All cabins with private facilities
(F) = Forward Cabin

GROUP	ACCOMMODATION	TYPE	DECK	FAR[E]
1	FOUR BERTH (F)	Inner	4/3	81
2	FOUR BERTH	Inner	4/3	89
3	FOUR BERTH	Inner	2	96
4	FOUR BERTH	Outer	2	106
5	THREE BERTH	Inner	4/3	105
6	THREE BERTH	Inner	2	11[ ]
7	THREE BERTH	Outer	3/2	12[ ]
8	TWO BERTH	Inner	4	12[ ]
9	TWO BERTH	Outer	3	14[ ]
10	TWO BERTH	Outer	2	15[ ]
11	TWO BEDDED	Inner	4/3	14[ ]
12	TWO BEDDED	Inner	2	16[ ]
13	TWO BEDDED	Outer	4/3	15[ ]
14	TWO BEDDED	Outer	2	17[ ]
15	SINGLE	Outer	3	220
16	SINGLE	Outer	2	235
17	DE LUXE	Outer	Boat	21[ ]
18	SUITE	Outer	Boat	239

EARLY SETTLER – SAVE 10% by paying full at time of booking which must be four months or more before departure. See p5[ ]

See – Money Savers p56/57, Deck Plan p[ ]
Booking and General Information p58-6[ ]

Azerbaydzhan, CTC Lines, 1975, 15,410grt, 157m x 22m, 21 knots. *Azerbaydzhan* cruised from Liverpool in 1993 to the Mediterranean and North Africa, returning to Dublin. She became *Arkadiya* in 1996, *Island Holiday* in 1997, and *Enchanted Capri* in 1998.

CTC CRUISE LINES
present
A 2-NIGHT PARTY CRUISE TO DUBLIN
◆ Saturday, 3rd - Monday, 5th September ◆

With Tom O'Connor *
& the Swing Section of The Geraldo Orchestra

* *Agreed at time of press*

CRUISE FROM LIVERPOOL
FROM ONLY
£99

Azerbaydzhan (1975/15,410grt) cruised from Liverpool to Dublin on 3 September 1994 and returned to Bristol on 5 September. Prices ranged from £99 for a 'friendly four' cabin to £259 in a deluxe suite on the boat deck.

Summer Sun from Liverpool & Bristol

8-15 night cruises

From only
£480

Southern Cross SC12

Liverpool for the Mediterranean
15 night cruise from £838
10-25 August '95

Cruising on *Southern Cross* is a sure way to see lots of places, enjoy the sunshine and have a great time. Start with two fascinating cities, Lisbon and Seville, then combine sightseeing with a lively time ashore in Gibraltar, Ibiza and Majorca. On the way back to the Mersey it's different again - the intriguing Arab world and bargain shopping in Morocco, Portugal's beautiful Algarve and the elegant Georgian squares of Dublin, with unscripted chat shows in countless famous pubs.

LIVERPOOL
Thu 10 Aug. Sails 1730 hrs
PORTIMAO (Portugal)
for Algarve Stay 11 hrs
Sun 13 Aug. Arr 1200 Dep 2300 hrs
GIBRALTAR Stay 15 hrs
Mon 14 Aug. Arr 0700 Dep 2200 hrs
IBIZA (Spain) Stay 15 hrs
Wed 16 Aug. Arr 0800 Dep 2300 hrs
PALMA (Majorca) Stay 14 hrs
Thu 17 Aug. Arr 0800 Dep 2200 hrs
CADIZ for Seville (Spain) Stay 14 hrs
Sat 19 Aug. Arr 0900 Dep 2300 hrs
TANGIER (Morocco) Stay 6 hrs
Sun 20 Aug. Arr 0800 Dep 1400 hrs
LISBON (Portugal) Stay 12 hrs
Mon 21 Aug. Arr 0800 Dep 2000 hrs
DUBLIN (Eire) Stay 10 hrs
Thu 24 Aug. Arr 0900 Dep 1900 hrs
LIVERPOOL Fri 25 Aug. Arr 0800 hrs

Seville - Spain (left) Ibiza (above)

Southern Cross SC13

Liverpool for the Islands
14 night cruise from £779
25 August - 8 September '95

After last year's success we have new ideas and places for 1995. The sights of Lisbon and its surroundings, the tax-free shopping of Gibraltar and Las Palmas, the beauty and friendliness of Madeira are essential. But this time you can sample the Moorish splendours of Granada or the sights of the Costa del Sol, the mysteries of old and modern Tangier in Morocco and the spectacular volcanic island of La Palma in the Canary Islands.

LIVERPOOL
Fri 25 Aug. Sails 1930 hrs
LISBON (Portugal) Stay 9 hrs
Mon 28 Aug. Arr 0900 Dep 1800 hrs
GIBRALTAR Stay 8 hrs
Tue 29 Aug. Arr 1400 Dep 2200 hrs
MALAGA (Spain)
for Granada Stay 16 hrs
Wed 30 Aug. Arr 0800 Dep 2400 hrs
TANGIER (Morocco) Stay 6 hrs
Thu 31 Aug. Arr 0800 Dep 1400 hrs
LAS PALMAS (Canary Is) Stay 14 hrs
Sat 2 Sep. Arr 0800 Dep 2200 hrs
**SANTA CRUZ DE LA PALMA
(Canary Is)** Stay 9 hrs
Sun 3 Sep. Arr 0800 Dep 1700 hrs
MADEIRA Stay 9 hrs
Mon 4 Sep. Arr 0900 Dep 1800 hrs
LIVERPOOL Fri 8 Sep. Arr 1000 hrs

Passengers land by launch or tender

DUBLIN • • LIVERPOOL
BRISTOL •
ST NAZAIRE For Nantes
CORUNNA BORDEAUX
VIGO •
• LEIXOES For Oporto LIVORNO For Pisa/Florence
LISBON •
PORTO SANTO PORTIMAO • CADIZ PALMA
• MALAGA • • IBIZA MAHON CIVITAVECCHIA For Rome
MADEIRA GIBRALTAR • • TANGIER
SANTA CRUZ DE LA PALMA CASABLANCA
SANTA CRUZ LANZAROTE
LAS PALMAS

Southern Cross (1972/17,042grt) cruised from Liverpool to the Mediterranean in 1995. *Southern Cross* was built as the *Spirit of London* for the P&O Line and was the first P&O passenger vessel to be built exclusively for cruising. She was built in Italy by C.N. del Tirreno & Riuniti, Riva Trigosa and was launched on 29 April 1972. P&O took over the contract for the vessel from the Norwegian Klosters Rederi and she sailed on her maiden voyage from Southampton to San Juan on 11 November 1972. Renamed *Sun Princess* in 1974, she became both *Starship Majestic* and *Southern Cross* in 1995. She is currently owned by Festival Cruises as *Flamenco*.

LIVERPOOL for the MEDITERRANEAN

≣ SOUTHERN CROSS SC39LL ≣

Liverpool
Wed 27 Aug Sails 1900 hrs

Lisbon (Portugal)
Sat 30 Aug Arr 1200 Dep 1900 hrs Stay 7 hrs

Tangier (Morocco)
Sun 31 Aug Arr 1400 Dep 2000 hrs Stay 6 hrs

⚓ **Villefranche for Monte Carlo (France)**
Wed 3 Sep Arr 0800 Dep 1800 hrs Stay 10 hrs

Malaga (Spain)
Fri 5 Sep Arr 1400 dep Sat 6 Sep 0200 hrs Stay 12 hrs

Gibraltar
Sat 6 Sep Arr 0800 Dep 1400 hrs Stay 6 hrs

Dublin (Eire)
Tue 9 Sep Arr 1300 Dep 1800 hrs Stay 5 hrs

Liverpool
Wed 10 Sep Arr 0500 hrs

⚓ Passengers land by launch or tender

MINI-CRUISE to DUBLIN & FRANCE

≣ SOUTHERN CROSS SC39LT ≣

Free coach from Liverpool or London City Centres

Liverpool
Wed 10 Sep Sails 1900 hrs

Dublin (Eire)
Thu 11 Sep Arr 0800 Dep 1800 hrs Stay 10 hrs

Le Havre for Paris (France)
Sat 13 Sep Arr 0700 Dep 1900 hrs Stay 12 hrs

Tilbury
Sun 14 Sep Arr 1000 hrs

Free coach back to London or Liverpool City Centres

Note: Inclusive coach service must be pre-booked. Coach booking forms will be forwarded with your Confirmation/Invoice.

Stop Dreaming • Start Cruising

CRUISE from LIVERPOOL

FROM ONLY

£240

CRUISE HOLIDAYS

at

Super Value Reader Offer Fares saving 20%

plus welcome cocktail party

CTC CRUISE LINES

Southern Cross cruise details for 1997.

The Union Castle liner *Windsor Castle* was built by Cammell Laird and sailed on her maiden voyage from Southampton to Cape Town and Durban on 18 August 1960. She was sold in 1977 to John Latsis and renamed *Margarita L*. She is presently laid up in Greece.

Two

Cargo Vessels

Shipping lines operated direct services for freight and other specialised cargos from the Port of Liverpool on a regular advertised conference basis. The Blue Funnel Line loaded at Vittoria Dock in Birkenhead for services to China, Hong Kong, Indonesia, Singapore and Thailand, and from Gladstone Dock in Liverpool for their services to Australian ports. Clan Line also operated from Vittoria Dock to South and East Africa, India, Pakistan and Ceylon.

The North Atlantic trade was served by the Cunard Line, Furness Warren Line, Lykes Lines and ships of the United States Lines. Ellerman's City, Hall and Papayanni lines loaded at both sides of the river and sailed to India, Pakistan, Aden and Mediterranean ports. Elder Dempster Line's vessels traded to most West African destinations while the Harrison Line traded to South Africa, South America and the West Indies. Blue Star Line's service ranged from the United States to Pacific Coast ports, Canadian, South African and New Zealand destinations and others jointly with the Lamport & Holt and Booth Lines.

Foreign flag vessels also provided services from the Port of Liverpool and included Nippon Yusen Kaisha Line's regular sailings to Japan, Nigerian National Shipping Line's sailings to West Africa, Pakistan Shipping Line and the Scindia Steam Navigation services to India and Pakistan.

City of Manchester, Ellerman-City Line, 1950, 7,583grt, 148m x 19m, 15½ knots. Sold in 1971 and renamed *Kavo Yerakes*, she arrived at Kaohsiung for breaking up on 11 November 1971.

On 1 October 1961 the *Journal of Commerce* celebrated its centenary as the major shipping newspaper of the UK. It was launched during a period of widespread industrial development and the extension of overseas trade; a period when trade with the British Empire was expanding and North Atlantic business was developing. The early editions of the *Journal of Commerce* recorded the Merseyside scene of the 1860s when there was tremendous shipping movements on the river accompanied by corresponding industrial activity in the docks. The first advertisement in the first column was for employment with the British & North American Royal Mail Steam Packet Co. and readers were asked to apply to Sir Samuel Cunard, Bart, Halifax. The line was the forerunner of the Cunard Line. In 1861 there were no Linotype or Inter-type machines and every page had to be hand set. Consequently, one finds few typographical errors in the early issues of the newspaper. It was not until 1886 that the first Linotype machine was installed in a New York newspaper and it was 1892 before a similar machine came to the *Newcastle Evening Chronicle*. The early issues featured advertisements for Thos. & Jas. Harrison; Bahr Behrend; William Inman; Allan Brothers; Imrie & Tomlinson and McDiarmid & Co. The *Journal of Commerce* moved from Castle Street to more extensive accommodation at 7-9 Victoria Street, Liverpool, in 1892. It continued to feature the popular columns on 'Mersey Extracts' and the arrivals and departure of vessels from the Port of Liverpool and some outports such as Gravesend, Queenstown, Dundee and Greenock. Charles Birchall, who purchased the paper in 1880, and his son Charles Herbert Birchall were responsible for the construction of and removal into the offices and factory block in James Street, Liverpool (shown above). By 1961 the company had become part of the Thompson Organisation and Charles Birchall remained as general manager until his retirement that year.

Print workers prepare an addition of the *Journal of Commerce*.

Blue Funnel Line vessels *Priam* (1966/12,094grt) and *Tantalus* (1945/7,712grt) unloading cargo at Gladstone Dock in 1967. *Priam* was sold in 1978 and renamed *Oriental Champion*. She was converted to a container ship in 1979 and broken up in 1985. *Tantalus* was built as *Macmurray Victory*, sold to Alfred Holt in 1946 becoming *Polyphemus*, and renamed *Tantalus* in 1960. She was sold in 1969, renamed *Pelops*, and broken up.

Cyclops, Blue Funnel Line, 1948, 7,688grt, 148m x 19m, 15 knots. She was renamed *Automedon* in 1975 and broken up at Dalmuir in 1977.

Atreus, Blue Funnel Line, 1951, 7,800grt, 148m x 19m, 16 knots. Renamed *United Valiant* in 1977, she was broken up at Kaohsiung in 1979.

Above: Elpenor, Blue Funnel Line, 1954, 7,757grt, 148m x 19m, 16 knots. She was renamed *United Concord* in 1978 and was broken up at Kaohsiung in 1979.

Blue Funnel Line's sailing details for 1961.

THE BLUE FUNNEL LINE
Alfred Holt & Co., India Buildings, Liverpool 2

AUSTRALIAN SERVICE HOMEWARD

SAIL   ARRIVE   JANUARY, 1961.

VESSEL	FINAL PORT		Genoa	Dunkirk	Antwerp	Liverpool	Glasgow	Other Discharge Ports
IXION	Sydney	Dec. 6	—	Jan. 3	Jan. 5	Jan. 8	Jan. 14	—
JASON	Brisbane	Jan. 3	—	Feb. 2	Feb. 4	Feb. 8	Feb. 15	—
NESTOR	Melbourne	Jan. 11	—	Feb. 9	Feb. 11	Feb. 15	Feb. 22	—
HELENUS	Fremantle	Feb. 4	—	Feb. 28	Mar. 2	Mar. 5	Mar. 11	—
NELEUS	Sydney	Feb. 11	—	Mar. 15	Mar. 17	Mar. 19	Mar. 25	—
HECTOR	Adelaide	Mar. 11	—	Apr. 7	Apr. 9	Apr. 12	Apr. 19	—
RHEXENOR	Sydney	Mar. 24	(Apr. 22)	(Apr. 27)	(Apr. 28)	Apr. 30	May 6	—

BLUE FUNNEL

When the new quota period for Hong Kong textiles begins on 1st February, 1961, there may be many Importers requiring earliest possible shipment and delivery of their goods.
To meet this, and to assist Importers in making early plans with their suppliers, Blue Funnel have arranged to have three vessels on the berth in the first half of February.

	AT HONG KONG	ARRIVES LIVERPOOL
Lycaon	27th January – 2nd February	6th March
Pyrrhus	5th February – 6th February	11th March
Anchises	12th February – 16th February	26th March

ALFRED HOLT & CO., INDIA BUILDINGS, LIVERPOOL 2. PHONE: CENTRAL 5630
BUTTERFIELD & SWIRE (HONG KONG) LTD., UNION HOUSE, 9 CONNAUGHT ROAD, HONG KONG. PHONE 35711

Achilles, Blue Funnel Line, 1957, 7,974grt, 150m x 19m, 16 knots. Renamed *Dardanus* in 1972, she was sold in 1973 and renamed *Kaigo* before being broken up in Calcutta in 1982.

Polydorus, Blue Funnel Line, 1952, 7,785grt, 148m x 19m, 16 knots. She was launched as *Alcinous* and renamed *Polydorus* in 1960. She became *Johara* and *Polydorus* again in 1976 and, after being sold in 1977, was renamed *Matina*. In 1979 she was broken up at Gadani Beach.

Myrmidon, Blue Funnel Line, 1980, 16,482grt, 165m x 26m, 18 knots. *Myrmidon* was renamed *Cape Town Carrier* in 1980 before reverting back to *Myrmidon* again in 1984. She was renamed *Bello Folawiyo* in 1988, *CMB Exporter* and *Merchant Promise* in 1989, *Lanka Amila* in 1990, *Merchant Promise* again in 1992 and *Tamamima* in 1993.

Oropesa, Pacific Steam Navigation Co., 1978, 14,124grt, 163m x 23m, 16 knots. She was sold in 1984 and renamed *Merchant Principal*, becoming *Lady Danielle* in 2000. She arrived at Alang to be broken up on 27 February 2001.

Booth Line

THE SUNNY WEST INDIES

BOOTH LINE

STEAMERS
"HUBERT"
"HILDEBRAND"
AND
"HILARY"

PROVIDE COMFORTABLE
FIRST AND TOURIST
CLASS ACCOMMODATION
TO

R.M.S. "HUBERT"
First-Class Double
Room with Bath

MARACAS BAY
By courtesy of
Trinidad and Tob-
ago Tourist Board

BARBADOS & TRINIDAD

VIA LEIXOES (OPORTO), LISBON and MADEIRA
and RETURN

EXCELLENT CUISINE
SPORTS DECK
SWIMMING BATH

For further particulars apply
to:—
BOOTH LINE
Cunard Building, Liverpool, 3

BLUE STAR LINE
London Passenger Representatives
3 Lower Regent Street,
London, S.W.1
or to Travel Agents

A COOLING DRINK
By courtesy of Barbados Publicity Committee

R.M.S. "HILDEBRAND"
Tourist Class Entrance

Hildebrand, Booth Line, 1951, 7,735grt, 134m x 18m, 14 knots. *Hildebrand* was built by Cammell Laird at Birkenhead in 1951 and sailed on her maiden voyage from Liverpool to Lisbon, Para and Manaus. She represented the Booth Line at the Coronation Review at Spithead on 15 June 1953. On 25 September 1957 she went aground outside Lisbon with 164 passengers on board. Two tugs attempted to refloat her but she was declared a total loss.

Scotia, Cunard Line, 1966, 5,850grt, 139m x 18m, 17½ knots. Sold in 1970 she was renamed *Neptune Amber*, becoming *Sri Kailash* in 1977. She was broken up at Bombay in 1984.

Above: Antrim, Avenue Shipping, 1962, 6,461grt, 140m x 18m, 14½ knots. She was renamed *Strathinch* in 1975, *Islami Taaj* in 1977, *Singapore* in 1980 and was broken up at Inchon in 1982.

Left: Hertford, Federal Steam Navigation, 1948, 11,276grt, 171m x 21m, 16 knots. She became *Thia Despina* in 1976, *Georgios Frangakis* in 1978 and, after having been laid up at Piraeus since 12 July 1977, was broken up at Aliga where she arrived by tow on 24 January 1985. She had never traded as *Georgios Frangakis*.

Outfit required

Cadets must have the following clothing and equipment in their possession on joining the Company.

ALL CADETS
1 Burberry style, Single Breasted Raincoat, Blue (R.N. pattern without belt).
1 Uniform Suit, Cloth (R.N. pattern), for shoregoing use, with 3 Company's Gold Buttons across cuffs.
1 Uniform Suit (R.N. pattern) for ship use, Battle-dress type, to take detachable shoulder straps.
1 White Mess Jacket.
1 Black wrap-round Cummerbund.
1 White Uniform Cap, Company's Badge and Band — best quality, for shore use.
1 White Uniform Cap, Company's Badge and Band — cheap quality, for ship use.
2 Uniform Black Ties.
1 Black Bow Tie.
2 Stiff White Collars.
4 Semi-stiff White Collars.
2 White Wing Collars.
1 Pair Uniform Brown Gloves (R.N. pattern).
1 Pair Uniform Shoes (R.N. pattern), no toe caps and no protectors.
1 Pair Working Shoes (no protectors) Black.
6 Pairs Black Socks.
1 Set Shoulder Straps with 3 small Company's gold buttons across.
4 White Uniform Shirts (without collars).
2 Pairs White Tropical Shorts (R.N. pattern).
2 White Tropical Shirts (R.N. pattern).
2 Pairs White Stockings (R.N. pattern).
2 Pairs White Socks.
1 Pair White Canvas Shoes.
2 Blue Working Shirts.
1 Pair Dark Grey Flannel Trousers.
1 Plain Navy Blue Double-breasted Blazer with Company Badge on pocket.
1 Pair White Gym Shoes.
2 White Gym Singlets.
2 Pairs White Gym Shorts.
1 Blue Tracksuit with small Company Badge.

DECK CADETS ONLY
1 Blue Boiler Suit.
2 Pairs Blue Dungaree Trousers.
1 Oilskin and Southwester.
1 Pair Rubber Sea Boots and Stockings.
2 Pairs Blue Working Shorts.
1 Plain Strong Leather Belt and Sheath Knife.

ENGINEER CADETS ONLY
2 White Unbleached Boiler Suits.
1 Pair Blue Dungaree Trousers.
1 Pair Blue Working Shorts.

The Company recommends that Cadets should also obtain the following optional items.
1 Pair Swimming Trunks.
2 Suits of Pyjamas.
3 Suits Lightweight Underwear.
1 Suit Heavy Underwear.
12 White Handkerchiefs.
1 Pair Braces.
1 Clothes Brush and usual toilet requirements.
Shoe Cleaning Gear for Black and White Shoes.
1 Housewife.
1 Canvas Kitbag or Hold-all.
1 Cabin Trunk (steel or fibre) or large suitcase.
1 Navy Blue Slipover (must not be visible when worn under Uniform Jacket).
1 Long Sleeved Navy Blue Guernsey.
1 Navy Blue Duffel Coat.
1 Pair Working Gloves.

Note: Civilian Clothing (Lounge Suits, Caps, etc.) must not form part of Cadet's outfit, though such items as an open necked shirt, old flannels or shorts may be worn on board below deck when off duty.

The Company's appointed outfitters are Monnery's Limited:
  5, Billiter Street, London, E.C.3.
  40, Oxford Street, Southampton.
  20, Water Street, Liverpool.

though all the above items may be obtained from any naval outfitters except for the Tracksuit and Company Badge for Blazer which Monnery's supply.

Towels, toilet soap, sheets, pillow cases and blankets are all provided by the Company.

A comprehensive stock of toilet requisites, confectionery and cigarettes is carried on all the Company's ships and a limited supply of clothing is also obtainable.

Washing machines and ironing facilities are provided on board for the use of all ranks.

When ordering outfit, due allowance should be made for individual growth.

Details of training schemes for navigating and engineer officer cadets in the New Zealand Shipping Co. in 1964.

HOW TO BECOME A

DECK or ENGINEER OFFICER

in

The New Zealand Shipping Company

(MEMBER OF THE P & O GROUP)

TRAINING SCHEMES FOR NAVIGATING AND ENGINEER OFFICER CADETS

Left: Nottingham, Federal Steam
Navigation, 1950, 6,689grt,
146m x 19m, 15 knots. She was
broken up in Taiwan in 1971.

Below: Sussex, Federal Steam
Navigation, 1949, 11,272grt,
171m x 21m, 16 knots. *Sussex*
was broken up at Hong Kong
in 1976.

Pipiriki, New Zealand Shipping Co., 1944, 10,065grt, 151m x 20m, 15½ knots. She was broken up at Kaohsiung in 1971.

Taupo, New Zealand Shipping Co., 1966, 10,983grt, 161m x 22m, 20 knots. *Taupo* was renamed *Mandama* in 1980 and broken up at Chittagong in 1984.

Left: Westmorland, Federal Steam Navigation, 1966, 11,011grt, 161m x 22m, 20 knots. She became *Fares Reefer* in 1980 and *Beacon Hill* in 1981. She arrived at Hyangpu from Jebel Ali, where she had been laid up since 5 July 1984, to be broken up.

Below: Tongariro, New Zealand Shipping Co., 1966, 10,980grt, 161m x 22m, 20 knots. After becoming *Reefer Princess* in 1979 and *Capetain Leonidas* in 1982, she was broken up at Gadani Beach in 1985.

Above: Leicestershire, Bibby Line, 1949, 8,908grt, 146m x 18m, 15½ knots. *Leicestershire* was built by Fairfield's at Glasgow and sailed on her maiden voyage on 21 January 1949 on Bibby Line's Burma service. She was sold in 1965 to Typaldos at Piraeus and was renamed *Heraklion*. In 1966 she capsized and sank on a voyage from Crete to Piraeus. Of the 281 people on board, only forty-seven survived.

Right: Warwickshire, Bibby Line, 1948, 8,903grt, 144m x 18m, 15½ knots. When the Bibby Line withdrew their passenger services in 1965 *Warwickshire* was sold to the Aegean Steam Navigation Co. and was converted to a car-ferry and sailed on the Piraeus-Crete service and renamed *Hania*. She was withdrawn in 1966, laid up in Greece and broken up.

Yorkshire, Bibby Line, 1960, 7,218grt, 150m x 20m, 16 knots. She was renamed *Eastern Princess* in 1963, *Yorkshire* again in 1964, *Bordabekoa* in 1971, *Sea Reliance* in 1981 and broken up at Alang where she arrived on 8 March 1984.

Cheshire, Bibby Line, 1959, 7,201grt, 150m x 20m, 16 knots. She was sold by Bibby Line in 1968 and renamed *Mozambique*, *Kota Mewah* in 1976 and broken up at Kaohsiung where she arrived on 24 August 1984.

Above: Derbyshire sailed on her maiden voyage on 8 November 1935 from Birkenhead to Marseilles, Colombo and Rangoon. She was converted to an Armed Merchant Cruiser in 1939 and later in the war she acted as a convoy escort and troop transport vessel. In 1942 she became an assault landing ship for the invasion of Sicily. She carried troops to Pechino in 1943 and Anzio and Southern France in 1944. In January 1945 she left Liverpool for Bombay and Ceylon as headquarters ship to General Mansergh taking troops back to Rangoon. She became the first troopship to berth at Singapore in September 1945 and the surrender of the Japanese was coordinated from her. *Derbyshire* was handed back to her owners in November 1947 after carrying 136,000 troops and steaming 330,000 miles. She was rebuilt by Fairfield's on the Clyde and returned to the Burma service. In 1964 negotiations took place to convert her to into an exhibition ship but the plan failed and she was broken up.

BIBBY LINE

M.V. "DERBYSHIRE"

BIRKENHEAD
TO
PORT SAID, PORT SUDAN, COLOMBO
AND

RANGOON

BERTH No. 222 WEST FLOAT, BIRKENHEAD
Telephone: CLAughton 2022

Commence Receiving:	Closing:
23rd DECEMBER, 1960	**3rd JANUARY, 1961**

Application for space should be made and completed Shipping Note lodged as early as possible with any of the undernoted Offices. Cargo is carried subject to all terms, conditions and exceptions of Shipping Notes, Wharfingers' Receipts and Bills of Lading.

Liverpool: **BIBBY BROTHERS & CO.,**
Martins Bank Building Water Street.   Telephone : CENtral 0492

London: **ALEXR. HOWDEN & CO. LTD.,**
107/112 Leadenhall Street, E.C.3.   Telephone : AVEnue 3444

LONDON to RANGOON
via Birkenhead

s.s. "WARWICKSHIRE"

Closing :   Sheds 11/12, TILBURY DOCK, 12th JANUARY, 1961
15th December, 1960

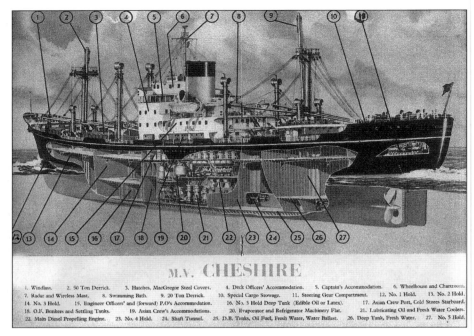

M.V. **CHESHIRE**

1. Windlass.   2. 50 Ton Derrick.   3. Hatches, MacGregor Steel Covers.   4. Deck Officers' Accommodation.   5. Captain's Accommodation.   6. Wheelhouse and Chartroom.
7. Radar and Wireless Mast.   8. Swimming Bath.   9. 20 Ton Derrick.   10. Special Cargo Stowage.   11. Steering Gear Compartment.   12. No. 1 Hold.   13. No. 2 Hold.
14. No. 3 Hold.   15. Engineer Officers' and (forward) P.O's Accommodation.   16. No. 3 Hold Deep Tank (Edible Oil or Latex).   17. Asian Crew Port, Cold Stores Starboard.
18. O.F. Bunkers and Settling Tanks.   19. Asian Crew's Accommodation.   20. Evaporator and Refrigerator Machinery Flat.   21. Lubricating Oil and Fresh Water Coolers.
22. Main Diesel Propelling Engine.   23. No. 4 Hold.   24. Shaft Tunnel.   25. D.B. Tanks, Oil Fuel, Fresh Water, Water Ballast.   26. Deep Tank, Fresh Water.   27. No. 5 Hold.

A cut-out view of Bibby Line's *Cheshire*, built by Cammell Laird in 1959.

Devonshire was built as a troop transport and spent the Second World War transporting troops to the Far East, Australia, South Africa and the Mediterranean. She was converted to a landing ship for the Infantry in 1943 and took part in the invasion of Sicily. In 1953 she was refitted and chartered to the Sea Transport Division of the Ministry of Transport and her base was transferred from Liverpool to Southampton. She was sold to the British India Line in 1962 and converted to an educational cruise ship and renamed *Devonia* to operate with Dunera. In this role she carried 190 first class and ninety-six second class passengers, and 830 students in dormitories. She continued in this role as an educational cruise vessel until 1967 when she was sold and broken up at Le Spezia.

Herefordshire, Bibby Line, 1944, 8,320grt, 150m x 20m, 15½ knots. She was launched as *Herefordshire* and was chartered and renamed *Port Hardy* in 1954, *Herefordshire* in 1961 and *Merryland* in 1969. She was broken up at Kaohsiung where she arrived on 2 February 1973.

Treneglos, Hain-Norse Line, 1963, 6,975grt, 154m x 20m, 15 knots. Renamed *Strathtrium* in 1975, *Siam Bay* in 1978, *Family Angel* in 1980 and *Doman* in 1984, she was broken up at Nantong in China where she arrived on 2 August 1985.

Hopepeak, Hopemount Steam Ship Co., 1963, 7,457grt, 153m x 20m, 15½ knots. She was renamed *Natalie* in 1969, *Pegasus* in 1981 and broken up at Xingang in China where she arrived on 10 May 1985.

Rembrandt, Bolton Steam Ship Co., 1960, 8,104grt, 150m x 19m, 13 knots. At the time of her construction *Rembrandt* was the highest powered free-piston, gas turbine-propelled vessel. It consisted of five free-piston gasifiers, four working and one standby, which supplied gas to a single non-reversing turbine. Transmission was through a locked-train double reduction gearing to a Stone-Kamewa controllable-pitch propeller. During the first year of service the propeller, turbine, gearing and auxiliaries performed almost faultlessly although there were minor problems with the gasifiers. The fact that she had a spare gasifier meant that maintenance was carried out at sea during the vessel's operational life.

Baron Maclay, H. Hogarth & Sons, 1959, 8,067grt, 142m x 18m, 13½ knots. She was renamed *Artagan* in 1968, *Sea Power* in 1977 and *Skyrian Hope* in 1981.

Ingleton, Chapman & Willan, 1960, 7,919grt, 138m x 18m, 14 knots. She was built as *Thistleroy* and became *Ingleton* in 1966, *Panetolikon* in 1970 and *Shabaan* in 1981.

Middlesex Trader (1963/14,083grt) prepares to swing in the river prior to entering the Birkenhead dock system in 1965. She became *Homer* in 1969, *Assios* in 1970, *Pollux* in 1978 and *Polo* in 1984. She arrived at the shipbreakers in Alang on 28 March 1985 after her delivery voyage from Tuticorin.

Glenmoor, Walter Runciman, 1953, 5,577grt, 137m x 18m, 13 knots. After being sold in 1976 and renamed *Saudi Fortune*, she was broken up at Chittagong in 1982.

Fourah Bay, Elder Dempster Line, 1961, 7,704grt, 142m x 19m, 16 knots. Became *Magda Josefina* in 1978, *Alexander's Faith* in 1980, *Lemina* in 1983, and was broken up at Gadani Beach where she arrived on 3 March 1984.

Photinia, Stag Line, 1961, 7,672grt, 146m x 18m, 13 knots. While waiting to berth at Milwaukee from Chicago on 13 May 1978 she was driven aground in a storm, stern first, after dragging her anchor. She was abandoned by Stag Line and sold to Selvick Maritime Towing and Midwest Marine Contractors who removed the machinery at Sturgeon Bay and towed her to Chicago in December 1978. She remained there for most of the following year and was towed to Kewaunee, Wisconsin where she arrived on 15 November 1979 for demolition by Baskins Bothers.

Perim, P&O Line, 1945, 9,550grt, 152m x 20m, 15½ knots.

The Cunard cargo vessel *Ivernia* (1964/5,586grt) arriving from New York and the *Cie des Messageries Maritimes Malais* (1959/7,475grt) in Sandon Dock in 1966.

Amarna, Moss Hutchison Line, 1949, 3,422grt, 112m x 16m, 14 knots. She was renamed *Assyria* in 1967, *Kastrian I* in 1976 and broken up in 1984.

Kypros, Moss Hutchison Line, 1950, 3,499grt, 112m x 16m, 13½ knots. Sold in 1967 and renamed *Aurania*, *Angeliki* in 1976, *Angel* in 1981, and broken up in India in 1982.

Above: Marabank, Bank Line, 1963, 6,249grt, 148m x 19m, 15 knots. Renamed *Good Lady* in 1978 and broken up at Chittagong where she arrived on 2 March 1985.

Left and below: Verdaguer, MacAndrews & Co., 1958, 2,049grt, 102m x 14m, 15½ knots. Became *Ursa* in 1971 and was broken up at Alang where she arrived on 26 December 1991.

Canadian Pacific

AMENDED

LIVERPOOL TO WEST SAINT JOHN N.B.

Through Bills of Lading to inland destinations in Canada and the United States

					Receiving Dates			
BEAVERCOVE	....	....	....	....	Feb.	15	—	Feb. 22
BEAVERFIR...	....	....	....	....	Feb.	25	—	Mar. 4
ROONAGH HEAD	....	....	....		Mar.	8	—	Mar. 13

LIVERPOOL TO QUEBEC AND MONTREAL

VESSEL (to be announced)....	....	....	Mar. 14	—	Mar. 18

LIVERPOOL TO TORONTO AND HAMILTON, DETROIT, CLEVELAND, *TOLEDO AND *SARNIA
*If sufficient inducement.

VESSEL (SCHULTE)	....	....	....	Mar. 22	—	Mar. 28

Loading Berth : North No. I Gladstone Dock

TO AVOID DELAY IN LOADING, shippers are advised to deliver their cargo as early as possible within the receiving date period, and to avoid the risk of short shipment, Customs Pre-Entry papers should be lodged either in advance of, or at the latest with, the goods at time of delivery at loading berth.

BILLS OF LADING must be presented by Shippers or agents not later than the day after closing.

INSURANCE at low rates.

GOODS ARE RECEIVED for shipment only subject to the terms and conditions of the Company's usual form of Wharfinger's Receipt and/or Bill of Lading.

CARGO OF HAZARDOUS NATURE can be accepted only by special agreement.

CANADIAN PACIFIC EXPRESS. Merchandise, samples, livestock and valuables sent by Express Service to all parts of Canada and the United States. When travelling, carry Canadian Pacific Express Travellers' Cheques.

Also Regular Service from London, Antwerp, Hamburg, Havre, etc.

For rates and other information apply :—
CANADIAN PACIFIC RAILWAY COMPANY
Royal Liver Building, Liverpool
Telephone: Central 5690
or to any other Canadian Pacific Office, a list of which is overleaf.
Subject to change without notice.

L.140 February 7th, 1963

Canadian Pacific Sailing List for February/March 1963.

Beaverford, Canadian Pacific Line, 1944, 9,881grt, 152m x 20m, 16 knots. She was built as *Empire Kitchener* and became *Beaverford* in 1946 and *Hulda* in 1962. On 18 August 1969 she was damaged by hurricane Camille and went aground at Gulfport, Mississippi, where she was declared a total loss.

Pacific Northwest, Furness Withy & Co., 1954, 9,442grt, 153m x 19m, 15½ knots. She was renamed *Aegis Power* in 1970 and was broken up in China in 1974.

RECEIVING AT No. 4 YORKHILL QUAY for	1960/1	JOINT ANCHOR-CUNARD SERVICE				1960/1
	Vessel	Receiving Belfast	Sails Glasgow	Arrives New York	Sails New York	Arrives Glasgow
NEW YORK BALTIMORE NORFOLK NEWPORT NEWS	BENNY SKOU	26th Oct.-3rd Nov.	5th Nov.	13th Nov.	25th Nov.	14th Dec.
	ALAUNIA (R)	9th-17th Nov.	19th Nov.	27th Nov.	9th Dec.	11th Jan.
	ASSYRIA (R)	23rd Nov.-1st Dec.	3rd Dec.	11th Dec.	23rd Dec.	25th Jan.
	BENNY SKOU	7th-15th Dec.	17th Dec.	25th Dec.	6th Jan.	22nd Jan.
	ALAUNIA (R)	21st-29th Dec.	31st Dec.	8th Jan.	20th Jan.	8th Feb.
	ANDANIA (R)	4th-12th Jan.	14th Jan.	22nd Jan.	3rd Feb.	22nd Feb.
	ASSYRIA (R)	18th-26th Jan.	28th Jan.	6th Feb.	17th Feb.	8th Mar.
	ARABIA	1st-9th Feb.	11th Feb.	20th Feb.		

NEW ORLEANS GALVESTON HOUSTON MOBILE TAMPA	As Loading Brokers for Cunard Steam-Ship Co. Ltd.					
	Vessel	Receiving Glasgow	Sails Glasgow	Arrives New Orleans	Sails Tampa	Arrives U.K.
	ASIA	3rd-11th Nov.	13th Nov.	7th Dec.	18th Dec.	1st Jan.
	IRISH LARCH	7th-13th Dec.	14th Dec.	29th Dec.	15th Jan.	30th Jan.

(R)—Refrigerated space available.

ANCHOR LINE

Elysia, Anchor Line, 1965, 6,499grt, 148m x 19m, 16 knots. She was renamed *Armanistan* in 1968, *Strathavoch* in 1975, *Sharp Island* in 1978 and broken up at Kaohsiung, where she arrived on 18 November 1983.

ANCHOR LINE

BOMBAY

ALSO

PORT SAID · SUEZ · ADEN

"ELYSIA"

CLOSING FOR CARGO

GLASGOW 12th JANUARY
YORKHILL QUAY

BIRKENHEAD 20th JANUARY
EAST QUAY, EAST FLOAT

TAKES CARGO FOR KANDLA (IF INDUCEMENT)

PORT SAID CARGO NOT ACCEPTED AT GLASGOW

Vessel has liberty to call at other U.K. Ports and at other Ports either on or out of route

Intending shippers wishing to ship cargo by this vessel should make application for space on the appropriate form which can be obtained and lodged at any of our offices.

Shipper must not despatch cargo to vessels until receipt of calling forward notice, and it is essential that shippers and suppliers should adhere to the delivery dates shown on such notices.

Goods insured on the most favourable terms.

All packages must be distinctly port marked.

All cargo received and shipped subject to terms and conditions of shipping notes, wharfingers receipts, and bills of lading.

December, 1960

Southern Venturer was owned by Chr. Salvesen & Co. and was one of the last three floating factory ships to participate in Antarctic whaling. In 1959/1960 *Belaena, Southern Harvester* and *Southern Venturer* were responsible for twelve per cent of the total Antarctic pelagic whaling catch. *Southern Harvester* was sold to Japanese interests in 1963 and the single land station at Leith Harbour at South Georgia was leased to a Japanese company resulting in a fundamental change in relative national stakes in Antarctic whaling. In 1939 there were nineteen expeditions under Norwegian and British flags, seven German expeditions and six operated by Japan. By 1948 the British and Norwegian fleets were still dominant, holding fourteen out of the nineteen expeditions, with the Dutch, Russians and Japanese joining the trade. Since 1931 Antarctic whaling has been subject to international regulation on both the species permitted to be caught and on minimum lengths. In 1945 the newly formed International Whaling Commission agreed an overall catch limit of 15,000 blue whales or equivalent. However, by the 1950s it was becoming evident that the stocks were being over-fished and catch levels were reduced. An agreement on new fishing levels was reached in 1962 as it was clear that stocks were falling dramatically. The sale of the British vessels broke a link with the tremendous amount of cooperation between Britain and Norway. The ships were managed by Britain but crewed by equal numbers of British and Norwegian sailors, who worked together in complete harmony.

Mersey Ore, Ore Carriers, 1960, 8,197grt, 149m x 20m, 15 knots. She was renamed *Garden Mars* in 1974 and left Chalkis on 11 August 1978 for Gandia in Spain to be broken up. She had been laid up at Chalkis since 28 January 1977.

Aldersgate, Bishopsgate Shipping Co., 1960, 12,718grt, 160m x 21m, 14 knots. She was sold and renamed *Silvershore* in 1969, *Puerto Madryn* in 1975, *Danube* in 1977 and was broken up at Chittagong where she arrived on 3 April 1984.

Manchester Commerce, Manchester Liners, 1963, 8,724grt, 153m x 19m, 17 knots. After being sold by Manchester Liners in 1971, she was renamed *Ber Sea* and *Yang Chun* in 1975. During the Iran/Iraq war she was seriously damaged by shelling and set on fire while berthed at Khorramshahr on 7 October 1980 and was declared a total loss.

Lindenbank, Bank Line, 1961, 6,234grt, 148m x 19m, 15 knots. On a voyage from Kimbe to European ports she went aground off Fanning Island on 17 August 1975 and became lodged in a coral reef. As she could not be re-floated she was declared a total loss.

Booker Vanguard, Booker Line, 1963, 5,417grt, 123m x 17m, 15 knots. She was sold in 1979 and renamed *Katy*, becoming *Franky* in 1981. She was sold by the Kenyan Admiralty Marshal to Graneco Maritime AB, Sweden, in 1984 and re-sold to Pakistan shipbreakers. After having been laid up at Mombassa since 24 November 1983, she left there in tow on 2 November 1984 for Karachi where she arrived on 27 November.

Harpalyce, J&C Harrison Ltd, 1958, 10,152grt, 165m x 19m, 13½ knots. Renamed *Patagonia* in 1972, *Efcharis* in 1974, *Intra Trophy* in 1982 and broken up at Cochin where she arrived on 12 April 1983.

Surrey Trader, Trader Navigation Co., 1964, 14,064grt, 178m x 23m, 14½ knots. She became *Saturn* in 1970, *Coraje* in 1978 and was broken up at Xingang in China where she arrived on 8 March 1985.

Right: Houlder Line advice for *Tewkesbury* sailing from South West, No.3 Alexandra Dock.

Below: Tewkesbury, Houlder Line, 1959, 8,532grt, 139m x 19m, 13½ knots. She was sold in 1972 and renamed *Caminito,* becoming *Brazil* in 1981. She left New Orleans on 4 June 1983 and arrived to be broken up at Busan in South Korea on 30 September.

SCHEDULE OF BASIC FARES

BETWEEN UNITED KINGDOM AND PRINCIPAL EASTERN PORTS

SUBJECT TO ALTERATION WITHOUT NOTICE

GRADE	PORT SAID	COLOMBO Homewards only	PENANG PORT SWETTENHAM AND SINGAPORE	BANGKOK	HONG KONG AND MANILA	KOBE AND YOKOHAMA
A1 per person	£68	£120	£180	£188	£194	£212
A/B per person	£63	£110	£165	£173	£179	£197
B2 per person	£55	£98	£145	£152	£157	£175

GRADES A1 Cabin in 'A' vessel with private bath or shower   A/B { Cabin in 'A' vessel without private bath or shower
B2 Cabin in 'B' vessel without private bath or shower   { Cabin in 'B' vessel with private bath or shower

NOTE Benreoch's single cabins are classified as B2 accommodation

RETURN TICKETS Passengers may obtain return tickets valid for one year. An allowance of 10 per cent off the sum of the two single fares is granted on these.

ROUND VOYAGES Enquiries for round voyages are welcome. Details of special concessionary fares will be supplied on application.

DETAILS OF VESSELS

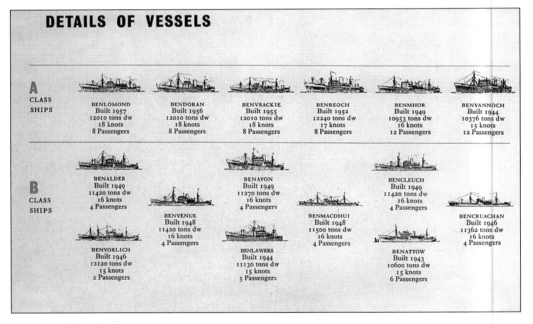

A CLASS SHIPS

BENLOMOND	BENDORAN	BENVRACKIE	BENREOCH	BENMHOR	BENVANNOCH
Built 1957	Built 1956	Built 1955	Built 1952	Built 1949	Built 1944
12010 tons dw	12010 tons dw	12010 tons dw	12240 tons dw	10953 tons dw	10376 tons dw
18 knots	18 knots	18 knots	17 knots	16 knots	15 knots
8 Passengers	8 Passengers	8 Passengers	8 Passengers	12 Passengers	12 Passengers

B CLASS SHIPS

BENALDER
Built 1949
11420 tons dw
16 knots
4 Passengers

BENAVON
Built 1949
11270 tons dw
16 knots
4 Passengers

BENCLEUCH
Built 1949
11420 tons dw
16 knots
4 Passengers

BENVENUE
Built 1948
11420 tons dw
16 knots
4 Passengers

BENMACDHUI
Built 1948
11500 tons dw
16 knots
4 Passengers

BENCRUACHAN
Built 1946
11362 tons dw
16 knots
4 Passengers

BENVORLICH
Built 1946
12120 tons dw
15 knots
2 Passengers

BENLAWERS
Built 1944
11130 tons dw
15 knots
5 Passengers

BENATTOW
Built 1943
10600 tons dw
15 knots
6 Passengers

Ben Line Schedule of Basic Fares and details of vessels operating in 1960.

Above: Benattow, Ben Line, 1951, 8,038grt, 153m x 20m, 15½ knots. She was built as *Cuzco* for the Pacific Steam Navigation Co. and became *Benattow* in 1965. She was broken up at Kaohsiung where she arrived on 25 September 1977.

Right: Benavon, Ben Line, 1949, 8,079grt, 147m x 18m, 15 knots. She was broken up at Kaohsiung in 1971.

NO FINER SERVICES FOR TRANS-ATLANTIC TRADE AND TRAVEL

A fine fast fleet of passenger and cargo vessels, headed by s.s. United States—the world's fastest liner—offers the following services:

FREIGHT Fast Services from British, German, Dutch, Belgian, French and Spanish ports to East Coast ports of U.S.A.

PASSENGER Trans-Atlantic luxury between the United Kingdom, Ireland, Germany, France and New York.

SUPER EXPRESS CARGO SERVICE
United States Lines' new 21 knot "Challenger" vessels provide super express services between London and New York and East Coast ports of U.S.A. and between Antwerp and Rotterdam and New York and U.S. East Coast ports.

HEAD FREIGHT OFFICE: 38 LEADENHALL STREET, LONDON E.C.3.   HEAD PASSENGER OFFICE: 50 PALL MALL, LONDON S.W.1

UNITED STATES LINES

United States Lines' passenger and cargo services in 1963.

American Traveler, United States Lines, 1946, 8,228grt, 140m x 19m, 16 knots. She became
Amercrest in 1970 and was broken up in 1972.

American Scientist, United States Lines, 1943, 8,239grt, 140m x 19m, 16 knots. She was built as
Sheridan and became *Messenger* and *American Scientist* in 1947 before being broken up in 1970.

Eugene Lykes, Lykes Line, 1945, 8,191grt, 140m x 19m, 15½ knots. She was launched as *Ocean Express* and was broken up at Kaohsiung where she arrived on 7 May 1970.

Mormachawk, Moore-McCormack Lines, 1945, 6,153grt, 140m x 19m, 16½ knots.

Kyvernitis, El-Yam Line, 1957, 10,300grt, 145m x 20m, 14 knots. She became *Platon* in 1973.

Kaderbaksh, Pakistan National Shipping Corporation, 1959, 8,991grt, 148m x 19m, 15 knots. In 1965 she was renamed *Gylfe* and was broken up at Karachi where she arrived on 6 October 1983.

Above: Indian Strength, India Steamship Co., 1958, 7,185grt, 155m x 20m 17½ knots. She became *Faulad Sardar* in 1980 and *Success* in 1982. On 11 January 1982 she was struck by two missiles when outward bound from Bandar Khomeini. She was abandoned by her crew after a fire broke out on the vessel and quickly spread.

Below: Indian Reliance, India Steamship Co., 1955, 7,422grt, 162m x 19m, 17½ knots. She was broken up in 1979.

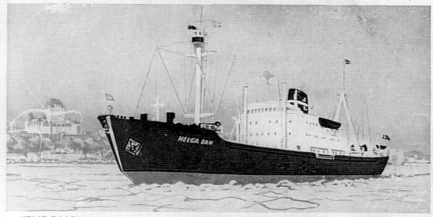

J. LAURITZEN Lines

(THROUGH BILLS OF LADING ISSUED TO INLAND DESTINATIONS)

LONDON and LIVERPOOL to QUEBEC
(WINTER SERVICE)

m.s. "HELGA DAN"
WILL SAIL FROM

LONDON, West India Dock, closing 31st December, 1960

LIVERPOOL, N. Gladstone Dock, closing 6th January, 1961

Pre-entry cargo tendered without Customs Papers is liable to be shut out and it is important that these documents be lodged at the loading berth not later than 24 hours after delivery of goods.

Hazardous cargo can be accepted only by special agreement.

Bills of Lading must be lodged not later than the day after vessel's closing date.

For Bill of Lading forms, rates of freight and all particulars, apply:

MARWOOD & ROBERTSON LTD.
18 WATER STREET, LIVERPOOL 2   Central 4271

J. A. FINZI, LAYMAN CLARK & CO. LTD.
34 LIME STREET, LONDON, E.C.3   Mansion House 3033

All cargo must be booked, and booking or acceptance is conditional upon the vessel named herein (if the vessel is named), or a suitable vessel being available for the voyage, and such booking or acceptance is subject to any direction or control of the vessel by any Government, or any other circumstances whatsoever which prevent the carriage of the cargo by the said vessel.

Cargo is received for shipment and carriage subject to all the clauses, conditions and exceptions contained in the form of Bills of Lading of the J. Lauritzen Lines. This form can be seen at the Offices of the Agents.

7th December, 1960

J. Lauritzen Line's sailing details for the winter service by m.s. *Helga Dan* from London and Liverpool to Quebec in 1961.

Vishva Jyoti, Shipping Corporation of India, 1959, 9,173grt, 154m x 20m 17 knots. She was launched as *Jala Vishva Jyoti* and became *Vishva Jyoti* in 1961.

Jalazad, Scindia Steam Navigation Co., 1955, 6,199grt, 152m x 19m, 15 knots. She was renamed *Jyoti Vinod* in 1981 and arrived at Tema on 23 December that year. In September 1983 she was lying abandoned and was scuttled off Tema.

Swat, National Shipping Corporation of Pakistan, 1958, 9,223grt, 149m x 19m, 15½ knots. She was built as *Wimbledon* and became *Port Wimbledon* in 1960, *Wimbledon* again in 1965 and *Swat* in 1968. She was broken up in Pakistan in 1982.

Oceantramp (1955/5,986grt) was launched as *Vigrafjord* and became *Oceantramp* in 1960, *Oriental* in 1970. She was abandoned after going aground fourteen miles south of Karachi on 26 June 1973 while on a voyage from China. She was declared a total loss by her owners.

Lebu, Cia Sud-Americana de Vapores, 1955, 8,679grt, 148m x 19m, 16 knots. While lying at Quintero Bay on 1 September 1973 she sustained serious engine room fire damage. She was towed to Valparaiso and sold to Spanish shipbreakers but, as she could not be delivered to the Spanish breakers in the stipulated time, she was resold to breakers at Split where she arrived on 22 October 1974.

COMPANIA SUD-AMERICANA DE VAPORES (C.S.A.V.)

Direct Service — Europe to PERU & CHILE

	Receiving from	Closing date	Berth BIRKENHEAD	DEPARTS	ARRIVES			
					Callao	Arica	Valpa-raiso	Talca-huano
m/v **Shropshire**	12th Dec.	19th Dec.	Shed 222, West Float	23rd Dec.	9/1/67	13/1/67	20/1/67	24/1/67
s/s **Andalien***	4th Jan.	11th Jan.	On application	16th Jan.	2/2/67	6/2/67	13/2/67	16/2/67

Accepting Cargo for Direct Delivery at — **Talara, Paita, Salaverry, Callao, Matarani, Ilo, Arica, Iquique, Tocopilla, Antofagasta, Chanaral, Coquimbo, Valparaiso, San Antonio, Talcahuano, San Vicente.**

Also if sufficient inducement or with Transhipment — **Chimbote, Eten, Pacasmayo, Pimentel, Chicama, Samanco, Cerro Azul, Pisco, Caldera, Huasco, Corral, Ancud, Puerto Montt, Castro, Puerto Chacabuco, Punta Arenas.**

*Refrigerated Space Available.

General U.K. Agents:
Vogt & Maguire Ltd.
Cross Keys House,
Moorfields, Liverpool 2
Telephone No. CENtral 9007/9 9000
Telegrams: VOGT Liverpool
TELEX 62/108

LONDON: VOGT & MAGUIRE LTD., Bevis Mark House, E.C.3. Tel. Avenue 7222/4. Telex 22665
GLASGOW: CONSTANTINE & CO. (Glasgow) LTD., 120 St. Vincent Street, C.2. Tel. City 6171. Telex 77-302
BIRMINGHAM: L. B. BLOXHAM & CO. LTD., 31 Colmore Row, 3. Tel. Central 4466/8.
BOSTON, LINCS.: READ & SUTCLIFFE LTD., 8 South Street. Tel. Boston 4242/3. Telex 37-509
CARDIFF: VOGT & MAGUIRE LTD., Dowlais Chambers, West Bute Street. Tel. Cardiff 28674
MANCHESTER: VOGT & MAGUIRE LTD., 20 Brazennose Street, 2. Tel. Blackfriars 4688

Date of Issue: 5/12/66

Compania Sud-Americana de Vapores' sailing list for December 1966.

Lotte Skou, Ove Skou, 1966, 4,829grt, 137m x 18m, 17½ knots. In 1978 she was sold and renamed *Huang Pu Jiang*

Nymphe, Virginiakmeth Cia.Nav.SA., 1954, 8,251grt, 146m x 19m, 16 knots. She was renamed *Virginia Methenitis* in 1970 and *Dryades* in 1977. On 4 December 1977 she went aground at Euboea Island on a voyage from Basrah to Volos and was abandoned.

River Andoni, Nigerian National Line, 1979, 10,983grt, 147m x 23m, 16 knots. *River Andoni* was placed under arrest and laid up at Ellesmere Port on 16 February 1994 before being sold and moved to dry dock at Birkenhead on 8 August 1996 for inspection and reconditioning. However, on 18 August she suffered a major fire in her engine room while in Bidston Dry Dock and was sold to Demtas A.S. of Turkey for demolition. She sailed in tow from Birkenhead for Aliaga on 22 December 1996 and, after arriving there on 7 January 1997, she was beached.

Herbert Macaulay, Nigerian National Shipping Line, 1957, 8,449grt, 140m x 18m, 13½ knots. Built as the *Sussex Trader*, she became *Herbert Macaulay* in 1964, *Anel D'Azur* in 1976 and was broken up in 1982.

SCINDIA
STEAM NAVIGATION CO. LIMITED

M/V	M/V
# JALAZAD	# JALADHARMA
LOADING FOR	LOADING FOR
KARACHI & BOMBAY	**MADRAS,**
(Refrigerated space available)	**CALCUTTA & CHITTAGONG**
	(Refrigerated space available)
Receiving Cargo at LONDON from	Closing for Cargo at GLASGOW
14th March	17th March, 1961
	LOADING BERTH TO BE ANNOUNCED
Closing 20th March, 1961	Closing for Cargo at BIRKENHEAD,
	24th March, 1961
LOADING BERTH:—No. 8 SHED	
GREENLAND DOCK	
SURREY COMMERCIAL DOCK	
(Swedish Yard Entrance)	**LOADING BERTH TO BE ANNOUNCED**

SUBJECT TO CHANGE WITHOUT NOTICE

Cargo must be booked with Freight Brokers by depositing the Shipping Notes in use
and Cargo must not be despatched until called forward by the Freight Brokers.

Gen. Agents:—SCINDIA STEAMSHIPS (LONDON) LTD.
KEMPSON HOUSE,
CAMOMILE STREET,
LONDON, E.C.3.   Tel. AVEnue 1200 (9 lines)
Telegrams: Jalanath, London
Freight Brokers for U.K.:—BAHR, BEHREND & CO., LTD.   Telex
INDIA BUILDINGS,
WATER STREET, **LIVERPOOL**   Tel. CENtral 4871
also at 123 MINORIES, **LONDON, E.C.3.**   Tel. ROYal 8361
INDIA HOUSE, 92 JOHN BRIGHT STREET,
BIRMINGHAM   Tel. MIDland 8716/7
YORKSHIRE BANK CHAMBERS, WILSON STREET,
MIDDLESBOROUGH   Tel. MID 45810
Glasgow Agents:—JOHN G. BORLAND & PEAT LTD.,
200 ST. VINCENT STREET, C.2.   Tel. CITY 3651
For Conditions of Carriage, Rates and other information apply to Local Agents (see overleaf)
March, 1961

Scindia Steam Navigation's sailing list for March 1961.

Yamashiro Maru, N.Y.K. Line, 1963, 10,466grt, 161m x 23m, 18 knots. After being renamed *Kyre* in 1974 and *Michele* in 1983, she was broken up at Alang where she arrived on 28 November 1983.

SAILING SCHEDULE
OF THE
N.Y.K. LINE TOKYO
(ESTABLISHED 1885)

INWARD   FAR EAST TO U.K. (LONDON & LIVERPOOL) & CONTINENT VIA SUEZ

Vessel	Dept. Japan	Dept. Keelung	Dept. Hong Kong	Dept. Singapore	Dept. Penang	Due Genoa	Due Marseilles	Due London	Due Liverpool	Due Antwerp	Due Rotterdam	Due Hamburg	Due Bremerhaven
* M.V. SATSUMA MARU ...	Feb 4	—	Feb 8	Feb 14	—	Mar 1	—	—	Mar 8	Mar 21	Mar 16	Mar 12	—
* M.V. AIZU MARU ...	Feb 17	Feb 21	Feb 23	Mar 2	—	Mar 21	Mar 23	Apr 3	—	Apr 7	Apr 1	Mar 30	—
* M.V. SHIZUOKA MARU ...	Mar 5	—	Mar 9	Mar 13	—	Mar 29	—	—	Apr 4	Apr 17	Apr 10	Apr 8	—
* M.V. AKI MARU ...	Mar 16	Mar 20	Mar 23	Mar 29	—	Apr 18	Apr 20	Apr 30	—	May 4	Apr 28	Apr 26	—
* M.V. SUMIDA MARU ...	Apr 2	—	Apr 6	Apr 11	—	Apr 28	—	—	May 4	May 17	May 11	May 9	—
* M.V. ATAMI MARU ...	Apr 16	Apr 20	Apr 23	Apr 29	—	May 19	May 21	May 31	—	Jun 4	May 29	May 27	—
* M.V. SURUGA MARU ...	May 2	—	May 6	May 11	—	May 28	—	—	Jun 3	Jun 17	Jun 11	Jun 9	—

* REFRIGERATED SPACE AVAILABLE

Samoa, East Asiatic Co. 1953, 8,628grt, 149m x 19m, 17 knots. Renamed *Parga* in 1976 and broken up in 1985.

Sinaloa, East Asiatic Co. 1956, 8,812grt, 150m x 20m, 17 knots. *Sinaloa* became *Yeun Chau* in 1978 and was broken up at Bangkok in 1983.

Dunkyle, St Andrews Shipping, 1957, 10,687grt, 154m x 21m, 12 knots. Renamed *Susie* in 1973, she was broken up at Aviles in 1979.

Tyne Ore, Ore Carriers, 1961, 12,232grt, 149m x 20m, 15 knots. Sold in 1975 and renamed *Rigote*, she became *Aninga* in 1975 and *Inga* in 1989. She was broken up at New Mangalore where she arrived on 3 February 1989.

Sheaf Wear, W.A. Souter & Co., 1959, 10,867grt, 153m x 21m, 12 knots. Renamed *Baltic Ore* in 1969, *Irish Wasa* in 1971 and *Christina* in 1977, she was broken up at Bilbao where she arrived in tow on 18 April 1977.

Arisaig, Scottish Ore Carriers, 1957, 6,872grt, 130m x 17m, 11 knots. Broken up at Faslane in 1972.

Rievaulx, Bolton Steam Ship Co., 1958, 10,974grt, 154m x 21m, 11½ knots. She was renamed *Silver Lake* and *Nema* in 1973. On 9 January 1984 she sailed from Osaka to be broken up in China, where she arrived on 15 January.

Dalhanna, Hunting & Son Ltd, 1958, 11,452grt, 154m x 21m, 12 knots. Renamed *Silver Island* in 1973 and *Amalia* in 1981, she was broken up at Gadani Beach in 1983.

Crania, Shell Tankers, 1955, 9,094grt, 153m x 21m, 12½ knots. She arrived at Kaohsiung on 3 May 1984 for breaking up.

Hemimactra, Shell Tankers, 1956, 12,278grt, 169m x 21m, 14½ knots. She was launched as *San Fortunato* and became *Hemimactra* in 1964. She was broken up at Kaohsiung in 1977.

Hyala, Shell Tankers, 1955, 12,164grt, 169m x 21m, 14½ knots. She was broken up at Kaohsiung in 1975.

Athelbeach, Athel Line, 1950, 7,533grt, 139m x 19m, 13 knots.

World Mead, Niarchos Group, 1953, 13,459grt, 170m x 23m, 15 knots.

Makeni Palm, Palm Line, 1951, 6,137grt, 129m x 17m, 11 knots. Launched as *British Rover*, she became *Makeni Palm* in 1961, *Kerkennah* in 1967, *Palau* in 1971, and was eventually broken up at Brindisi where she arrived on 11 June 1978.

Esso Purfleet, Esso Petroleum, 1967, 2,838grt, 99m x 15m, 11½ knots. She was renamed *Prima Jemima* in 1983, *Thita Pegasus* in 1986, *Rainbow* and *Dubai Star* in 1987, *El Miura* in 1991 and *Sicily* in 1995.

Edward Stevinson, Stevinson Hardy & Co., 1961, 31,317grt, 230m x 30m, 15½ knots. She was broken up at Kaohsiung in 1981.

The Shell tanker *Serenia* (1961/42,082grt) in Grayson Rollo & Clover's newly enlarged No.1 Dock in 1961. The overhang of the bow allowed the 249m vessel to enter the 244m-long dock. *Serenia* was laid up at Labuan in 1975 and was moved in 1977 for North Sea work. She was converted by Rhine-Schelde-Verolme at Rotterdam for off-shore oil loading and was employed in the North Sea until 1987 when Shell purchased the Norwegian tanker *Gerina* (1980/65,173grt) to replace her. She left the Mersey on 10 July and arrived at Kaohsiung on 4 September 1987 to be broken up.

Sepia, Shell Tankers, 1961, 42,109grt, 249m x 34m, 16 knots. In April 1975 *Sepia* arrived at Brunei Bay, south of Labuan at the eastern side of the South China Sea to lay up due to the depressed state of the price of oil. In 1977 she was used to lighten tankers off the Mississippi entrance, unloading oil from tankers for delivery to Garyville Refinery on the river. She had been laid up at Labuan with her sister *Serenia*, which was moved in 1977 for North Sea work. *Sepia* was sold for scrapping at Kaohsiung where she arrived on 30 August 1983.

Three
Coastal Vessels

The Port of Liverpool has always been the main gateway for trade to Ireland. Coast Lines were the main shipping operator for coastal services to Belfast, Dublin and other smaller Irish ports. The Belfast Steamship Co. provided both freight and a nightly passenger service to Belfast, while the British & Irish Steam Packet Co. vessels sailed to Dublin. In 1963 there were more than ten services from the Mersey to Dublin, Belfast and other Irish ports and over 500,000 people travelled across the Irish Sea between Liverpool and Belfast and Liverpool and Dublin.

Ships of the Isle of Man Steam Packet provided a daily passenger service to Douglas, Isle of Man, throughout the year and their main freight service via the company's cargo vessels.

Most of this cargo had been carried by conventional vessels but by 1963 there was a steady growth in the shipment of cargoes in unit loads and containers. Link Line's *Wirral Coast* pioneered this business in 1962 when she inaugurated a service from Liverpool to Dublin before being replaced by the larger capacity *Terrier* in 1963. The Link Line service from Liverpool to Belfast began in 1959 and by 1963 it was so well supported that two new vessels, *Buffalo* and *Bison*, were introduced and new facilities were provided at North Trafalgar Dock to deal with the unit load traffic.

When the south dock system was closed in 1972, the Isle of Man Steam Packet sold their conventional freight vessel, *Fenella*, and chartered *Spaniel* from the Belfast Steamship Co. They had her adapted for the carriage of containers, sold the smaller *Ramsey* and converted the *Peveril* to a container vessel in 1972.

Conventional passenger vessels were sold and replaced by purpose-built car ferries for the Dublin, Belfast and Douglas services. Several of the older passenger ships were purchased by Greek owners and converted to cruise in the Mediterranean.

Ben-My-Chree II (1927/2,586grt) prepares to leave Morpeth Dock on 18 December 1965 to be broken up at Ghent.

Details of *Fiesta* cruises to Greece, Turkey, Cyprus and Israel. *Fiesta* was built as *Mona's Queen* for the Isle of Man Steam Packet and was sold in 1962 and renamed *Barrow Queen* and *Carina* in 1963 when she was converted for cruising. In 1964 she became *Fiesta* and carried out various cruising programmes in the Mediterranean until 1981 when she was broken up at Piraeus.

Fiesta

15-day cruises to Greece, Turkey, Cyprus and Israel

	15-day cruises				17-day Easter cruise		
Prices are per person from London back to London **No 'V' Form** Category, deck and type of cabin	S.A.M. Special Flight Caravelle Jet	British Eagle One-Eleven Jet Day Flight**	B.E.A. Alitalia Weekend Day Flight*	Train 2nd class†	S.A.M. Special Flight Caravelle Jet	B.E.A. Alitalia Weekend Day Flight	Train 2nd class†
Emerald Deck	Gns	Gns	Gns	Gns	Gns	Gns	Gns
W1 Four-berth inside with shower and toilet	91	93	119	93	103	131	105
W2 Two-berth inside with shower and toilet	116	118	144	118	128	156	130
W3 Two-bed inside with shower and toilet	128	130	156	130	140	168	142
Ivory Deck							
X1 Four-berth inside with shower and toilet	100	102	128	102	112	140	114
as three-berth	125	127	153	127	137	165	139
as two-bed	150	152	178	152	162	190	164
X2 Four-berth outside with shower and toilet	115	117	143	117	127	155	129
as three-berth	145	147	173	147	157	185	159
as two-bed	175	177	203	177	187	215	189
X3 Two berth inside with shower and toilet	135	137	163	137	147	175	149
X4 Two-berth outside with shower and toilet	157	159	185	159	145	173	147
X5 Two-bed inside with shower and toilet	163	165	191	165	151	179	153
X6 Three-berth outside with shower and toilet	168	170	196	170	156	184	158
X7 Two-bed outside with shower and toilet	187	189	215	189	175	203	177
Coral Deck							
Y1 Two-berth inside with wash basin	137	139	165	139	125	153	127
Y2 Two-berth outside with wash basin	143	145	171	145	131	159	133
Y3 Two-berth inside with shower and toilet	157	159	185	159	145	173	147
Y4 Two-berth inside with shower and toilet	168	170	196	170	156	184	158
Y5 Two-bed inside with shower and toilet	172	174	200	174	160	188	162
Y6 Two-berth outside with shower and toilet	187	189	215	189	175	203	177
Y7 Two-berth outside with bath and toilet	197	199	225	199	185	213	187
Y8 Two-bed outside suites with sitting room, bathroom and toilet	252	254	280	254	240	268	242

Port Taxes. £4.15s. per person extra (children under 12 years of age at date of sailing £2.7s.6d.)
High Season Cruise Supplement for all sailings in July, August and September £5.5s. per person (£2.12s.6d. for children sharing parents' cabin)
*These air prices are increased by £4.4s. for all departures between June 16 and September 30.
†Supplement for first class rail travel £12.19s.
**The One-Eleven Jet flights from London, Heathrow Airport, will be operated in connection with all sailings from May 17 to September 20, and will include lunch and sightseeing in Venice.
A One-Eleven Jet direct flight from Manchester will be operated in connection with all sailings from May 17 to September 20. Add £4.4s. to the One-Eleven fares from London. Passengers may join and leave the cruise at Venice at a reduction of £17.17s. off the S.A.M. Special Flight price.
For Travel Information see page 21.
Credit Vouchers may be purchased for an amount equivalent to 20% of the cruise fare but not exceeding £50 per person and may be used for expenses on board. They are issued in denominations of £2.

tss Fiesta

Practically all cabins on this one class ship have private facilities. There is plenty of sun-deck space, a fine tiled swimming pool, a very attractive lounge and dance floor, a panoramic dining room, bars, beauty salon and duty free shop at the disposal of the limited number of passengers who are able to obtain accommodation on this intimate one-class cruise vessel.

Vital Statistics:

Length 347 feet; Breadth 47 feet; No. of Decks, 5 (Sun, Promenade, Coral, Ivory, Emerald); Speed 20 knots; G.R.T. 3500 tons (approx); Radio Signal, FIESTA SYQN; Voltage 220 D.C.; Builders, Cammel Laird & Co. Ltd., Birkenhead. Classified ✠ 100 A1 at Lloyd's Register of Shipping in London.

FIESTA

Greece, the Greek Isles, Turkey and the Dalmatian Coast
15-Day Cruises from 107 gns to 257 gns London back to London

Sailing dates: March 28 ; April 11, 25 ; May 9, 23 ; June 6, 20 ; July 4, 18 ; August 1, 15, 29 ; September 12, 26 ; October 10.

Saturday	Gatwick	Depart about 9.15 a.m.
	Venice	Embark. Sail at 10.0 p.m. Dinner on board.
Sunday	At Sea	Cruising in the Adriatic.
Monday	Corfu	Arrive morning. Sail early afternoon. Optional excursion. Approximate time in port 6 hours.
Tuesday	Athens	Arrive early morning. Sail early afternoon. Optional excursion, shopping. Approximate time in port 10 hours.
Wednesday	Chios	Arrive early morning. Sail early afternoon. Optional excursion. Approximate time in port 6 hours.
Thursday	Istanbul	Arrive early morning. Sail evening. Optional excursion. Approximate time in port 10 hours.
Friday	Kusadasi	Arrive afternoon. Sail at night. Optional excursion to *Ephesus*. Approximate time in port 6 hours.
Saturday	Rhodes	Arrive morning. Sail at night. Optional excursions. Bathing, shopping. Approximate time in port 14 hours.
Sunday	Heraklion	Arrive morning. Sail at noon. Optional excursion to *Knossos*. Approximate time in port 4 hours.
	Santorini	Arrive afternoon. Sail late evening. Optional excursion to *Thera*. Approximate time in port 5 hours.
Monday	Delos	Arrive morning. Sail forenoon. Optional excursion. Approximate time in port 4 hours.
	Mykonos	Arrive midday. Sail evening. Bathing, shopping, sightseeing. Approximate time in port 9 hours.
Tuesday	Athens	Arrive early morning. Sail midnight. Optional excursions. Shopping, bathing. Approximate time in port 18 hours.
Wednesday	Itea	Arrive morning. Sail early afternoon. Optional excursion to *Delphi*. Approximate time in port 6 hours.
Thursday	Kotor	Arrive early afternoon. Sail late night. Optional excursions. Shopping, bathing. Approximate time in port 8 hours.
Friday	Dubrovnik	Arrive early morning. Sail noon. Optional excursion. Approximate time in port 5 hours.
Saturday	Venice	Arrive 8.0 a.m. Disembarkation after breakfast.
	Gatwick	Arrive about 2.0 p.m.

Cruise details for *Fiesta*'s fifteen-day cruises to the Greek Islands, Turkey and the Dalmation Coast from 107 guineas to 157 guineas.

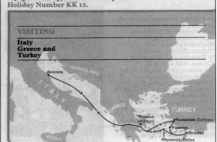

Odysseus was launched as *Leinster* for the B&I line's service from Liverpool to Dublin. She was transferred to the Belfast route in 1946 and renamed *Ulster Prince*. In 1966 she was replaced by a new car-ferry of the same name and she became *Ulster Prince I*. She became *Adria* after being sold to the Epirotiki Steam Ship Co. in 1968 and *Odysseus* in 1969. She arrived at Glasgow on 22 July 1977 to be laid up and was sold to Shipbreaking Industries at Faslane where she arrived on 2 October 1979.

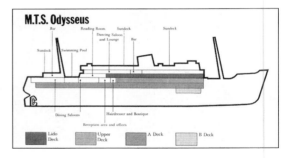

Scottish Coast (1957/3,817grt) was built for Burns & Laird and also acted as relief vessel on Coast Line's various routes when the normal vessel was undergoing annual overhaul. She was sold in 1968 and was renamed *Galaxias* for use as a cruise ship in the Mediterranean, becoming *Princesa Amorosa* in 1989. She was sold in 2002 for demolition in Turkey.

DECK PLANS

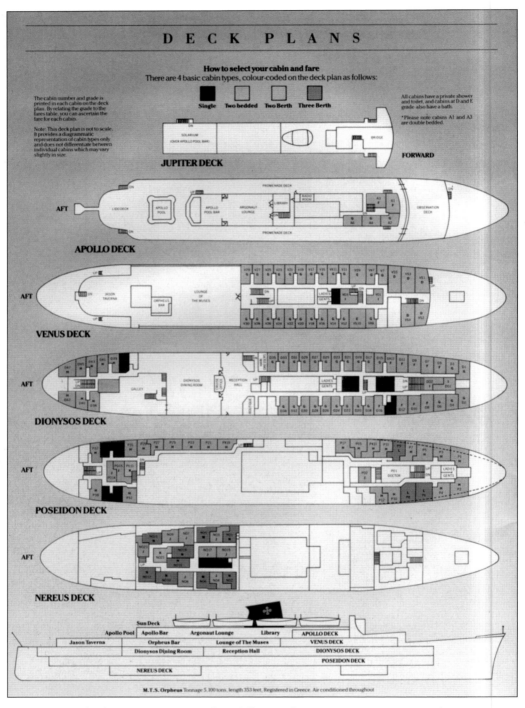

Deck plans for *M.T.S. Orpheus* following her conversion to a cruise ship.

Ulster Monarch (1929/3,815grt) berths at Princes Landing Stage from Belfast while *Manxman* (1955/2,495grt) prepares to sail to Douglas, Isle of Man.

Ulster Queen (1967/4,270grt) passes *St Clair* (1969/3,303grt) in Princes Dock as she returns from her annual overhaul. *St Clair* had operated the Liverpool to Belfast sailing while *Ulster Queen* and *Ulster Prince* were undertaking their overhaul in 1970. She was replaced on the Aberdeen to Lerwick service by *St Ninian* (1950/2,244grt) while *St Clair* was in the Irish Sea.

LIVERPOOL
DAILY POST

COAST LINES SUPPLEMENT
WEDNESDAY, APRIL 19, 1967

Bon voyage!

TONIGHT, the new BELFAST STEAMSHIP CO. LIMITED ferry ship ULSTER PRINCE sails from LIVERPOOL to BELFAST on her maiden voyage and so inaugurates the first ever passenger and drive-on/drive-off ferry between the two cities. Soon she will be joined by ULSTER QUEEN, and together they will operate every weeknight and, additionally, every Sunday during the period 9th July—17th September.

Whether travelling on business or on holiday, First or Second Class, this is the overnight route for the discerning passenger from city centre to city centre. De Luxe suites, cabins and sleeping berths, lounges, restaurants, cafeterias and bars.

If you are not taking your car, there are now fast electric train connections between Liverpool, London and the Midlands.

And remember, there are **NO CURRENCY RESTRICTIONS** in travelling to and from Northern Ireland.

Ulster Prince (1967/4,270grt) prepares to sail on her maiden voyage at Princes Dock on 19 April 1967. She remained on the Liverpool to Belfast service until 1982 when she was sold and renamed *Lady M*, *Tangpakorn* in 1984, *Long Hu* and *Macmosa* in 1988, *Neptunia II* and *Neptunia* in 1995, *Panther* in 1996, *Vatan* in 2000 and *Manar* in 2001.

Ulster Queen passes Seacombe Landing Stage and prepares to turn in the river to dock at Waterloo Dock as B&I's *Leinster* moves astern out of Waterloo Lock.

St Edmund was built in 1974 by Cammell Laird for British Rail's Harwich to Hook of Holland service which she covered until 1975 when she was sold to Pastruck (Shipping) and chartered back to British Rail. In 1982 she was chartered to the Ministry of Defence to transport troops to the Falkland Islands, while also being used as a troop carrier from the Ascension Islands to Port Stanley as the new airport had not been completed. It was in this role that she was also used to carry Argentinean prisoners of war, including General Menendez, to Puerto Madryn. During this time she was renamed *Karen*. By 1985 she had completed twenty-seven voyages and carried 18,000 troops and workers. She was laid up and sold to Cenargo that year and renamed *Scirocco*. The following year she was chartered to Tirrenia Line of Italy and operated on the Tunisian State Line, Cotunav, between Tunis to Marseille and Genoa. Renamed *Rozel* in 1989 to operate on the Poole to Channel Islands service for British Channel Islands Ferries, she was renamed *Scirocco* again in 1994 for Cenargo's Almeria to Nador, Morocco service, eventually being replaced on this route by *Esterel* in 1997. However, in 2003 she was on Ferrimaroc's service between Almeria and Nador in Morocco.

Now! The B+I Line can book you and your car and caravan through to Nine European countries and home again, at special reduced through rates

Just drive aboard at the new B+I Ferryport in Dublin and off again at Liverpool. A drive through Britain—full of interest-brings you to the British port where you drive aboard for Europe and any one of the international ports which are the gateways to your chosen holiday country. And remember, through the B+I Continental Service, you can plan your holiday so that you travel out one route and return by another and still have the advantage of reduced through rates.

The best way to take your car is by the newest, fastest and most luxurious ship on the Irish Sea — by B+I Motorway. You can go by day or night crossings and there are ten a week to choose from during the peak holiday season. Of course if you do not wish to take your car, any B+I office can provide through bookings, including rail or coach travel. There are many tours and inclusive holidays of all kinds, in all the European Countries. Ask us for brochures and details.

We are proud to have been appointed Official Agents by these world renowned shipping companies.

BERGEN LINE	FINNLINES
DFDS LINE	TOWNSEND FERRIES
ENGLAND/SWEDEN LINE	THORESEN CAR FERRIES
TOR LINE	SWEDISH LLOYD
PRINS FERRIES	GOTHENBURG– FREDERIKSHAVN LINE
TRAVE-LINE	NORTH SEA FERRIES

In conjunction with their services we can offer a most economical and comprehensive range of through passenger and car facilities for travel to all the countries of Western Europe.

B+I Motorway. So easy ... So convenient ... So economical

B&I Motorway and B&I Continental booking service for sailings in 1968.

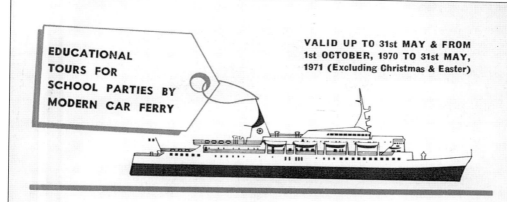

EDUCATIONAL TOURS FOR SCHOOL PARTIES BY MODERN CAR FERRY

VALID UP TO 31st MAY & FROM 1st OCTOBER, 1970 TO 31st MAY, 1971 (Excluding Christmas & Easter)

★ **Visit Dublin, Capital City of Ireland and its renowned Zoo.**

★ **Explore Glendalough, Ireland's Ancient Ecclesiastical Settlement.**

★ **Enjoy a 100 mile tour by coach.**

Educational Tours by B+I Motorway allow Students a full day in Ireland.

ITINERARY :

22.15 hrs.	Depart B+I Ferryport, LIVERPOOL. Tour of Car Ferry, including visit to bridge.
07.00 hrs.	Arrive DUBLIN.
08.00 - 10.30 hrs.	Coach tour of DUBLIN, including a visit to Trinity College.
10.30 - 12.30 hrs.	Free time for shopping.
12.30 - 15.00 hrs.	Visit to the Zoological Gardens where lunch is provided.
15.00 - 21.00 hrs.	Coach tour via the Scalp, Enniskerry and Roundwood, to Glendalough, returning via Rathdrum and Rathnew to Ashford for tea. Later continue by way of seaside resorts of Bray, Killiney and Dun Laoghaire to B+I Ferryport, DUBLIN.
22.15 hrs.	Car Ferry departs.
07.00 hrs.	Arrival at B+I Ferryport, LIVERPOOL.

This itinerary can be adjusted to suit individual requirements. All arrangements must be made in advance.

RETURN FARE 75/- (Includes Return Fare, Coach Tours, Two Meals and Entry to Zoo. Berths and Meals on Car Ferry are not included.)

ENQUIRIES SHOULD BE ADDRESSED TO :

 Reliance House, Water Street, Liverpool, L.2. 8 T.S.

Telephone 051-236-5464.

John T. Drought, Ltd., Printers, Dublin, 1.

Educational tours for school parties by B&I Line from Liverpool to Dublin in 1970/1971.

101

Saint Patrick II, Irish Ferries, 1973, 7,984grt, 126m x 22m, 21 knots. She was built as *Aurella* becoming *Saint Patrick II* in 1982, *Egnatia II* in 1998 and *City of Cork* in 2000.

Lion, Burns & Laird Line, 1967, 3,333grt, 111m x 17m, 20½ knots. She was renamed *Baroness M* in 1985, *Portelet* in 1987 and *Baroness M* again in 1988.

Saint Colum I, Belfast Ferries, 1973, 5,284grt, 118m x 18m, 22 knots. She was built as *St Patrick* and renamed *Saint Colum I* in 1982, *Dimitrios Express* in 1990, *Kadia Express* in 1993 and *Poseidon Express II* in 1996.

Viking II (1964/3,660grt) became *Earl William* in 1977 and was operated on the new Sealink Liverpool to Dun Laoghaire service in 1988. She was laid up and sold in 1992, becoming *William, Pearl William* and *Mar Julia* in 1996, *Cesme Stern* in 1997 and *Windward II* in 2002.

Coast Line's *Irish Coast* (1952/3,824grt) berths in the south lock at Alfred Dock, Birkenhead, in 1968. She was laid up in Morpeth Dock while she was for sale and was renamed *Orpheus* when sold later that year. She became *Semiramis II*, *Achilleus* and *Apollon II* in 1969 and *Regency* in 1981. She was broken up in 1989.

The first fastcraft to operate from Merseyside was the British Midland hovercraft which inaugurated a service between Leasowe in Wirral and Rhyl in North Wales on 20 July 1962.

Innisfallen, City of Cork Steam Packet Co., 1948, 3,705grt, 104m x 15m, 17 knots. Renamed *Innisfallen I* and *Poseidonia* in 1969, she was broken up at Brindisi in 1985.

Ionic Ferry was originally *Dragon* operating from Southampton to Le Havre by Southern Ferries. She was transferred to the Larne to Cairnryan route in 1986, becoming part of P&O European Ferries Group in 1987. Sold in 1992, she became *Viscountess* M and *Charm* M in 1996 and *Millennium Express II* in 1999. In 2002 she suffered a serious engine room fire on a sailing from Greece to Albania and was towed to Eleusis in Greece where she was surveyed and laid up.

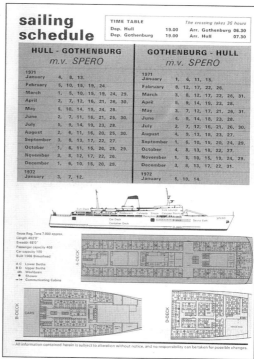

sailing schedule

TIME TABLE		The crossing takes 36 hours	
Dep. Hull	19.00	Arr. Gothenburg	06.30
Dep. Gothenburg	19.00	Arr. Hull	07.30

HULL - GOTHENBURG m.v. SPERO		GOTHENBURG - HULL m.v. SPERO	
1971		**1971**	
January	4, 8, 13.	January	1, 6, 11, 15.
February	5, 10, 15, 19, 24.	February	8, 12, 17, 22, 26.
March	1, 5, 10, 15, 19, 24, 29.	March	3, 8, 12, 17, 22, 26, 31.
April	2, 7, 12, 16, 21, 26, 30.	April	5, 9, 14, 19, 23, 28.
May	5, 10, 14, 19, 24, 28.	May	3, 7, 12, 17, 21, 26, 31.
June	2, 7, 11, 16, 21, 25, 30.	June	4, 9, 14, 18, 23, 28.
July	5, 9, 14, 19, 23, 28.	July	2, 7, 12, 16, 21, 26, 30.
August	2, 6, 11, 16, 20, 25, 30.	August	4, 9, 13, 18, 23, 27.
September	3, 8, 13, 17, 22, 27.	September	1, 6, 10, 15, 20, 24, 29.
October	1, 6, 11, 15, 20, 25, 29.	October	4, 8, 13, 18, 22, 27.
November	3, 8, 12, 17, 22, 26.	November	1, 5, 10, 15, 19, 24, 29.
December	1, 6, 10, 15, 20, 29.	December	3, 8, 13, 17, 22, 31.
1972		**1972**	
January	3, 7, 12.	January	5, 10, 14.

Gross Reg. Tons 7.000 approx.
Length 452'0"
Breadth 68'0"
Passenger capacity 408
Car capacity 100
Built 1966 Birkenhead

A C Lower Berths
B D Upper Berths
⊕ Washbasin
● Shower
←|← Communicating Cabins

All information contained herein is subject to alteration without notice, and no responsibility can be taken for possible changes.

Spero was built by Cammell Laird at Birkenhead in 1966 for Ellerman's Wilson Line service from Hull to Gothenburg. She operated briefly to Zeebrugge in 1972 and was sold and renamed *Sappho* by her new Greek owners. She is 6,916grt and was designed to carry 950 passengers and 250 cars. In 2002 she was sold to Lacerta Shipping (Tanzania) Ltd and was renamed *Santorini 3*.

Caledonian Coast, Coast Lines, 1948, 1,265grt, 84m x 12m, 14 knots. She was chartered by the Brocklebank Line in 1967 and renamed *Makalla* and *Ahmadi Coast* in 1968. She was broken up at Cartagena in 1974.

Ocean Coast (1935/1,173grt) was originally built as *Anglian Coast*. She was owned by Coast Lines for most of her life becoming *Effy* in 1964 and *Anna Maria* in 1967. On 8 February 1969 she went aground off Constanza and was abandoned by her crew.

Kentish Coast, Coast Lines, 1946, 498grt, 61m x 9m, 12 knots. Built as *Ulster Duchess*, she was renamed *Jersey Coast* in 1946, *Ulster Weaver* in 1954 and *Kentish Coast* in 1964. She became *Salimiah Coast* in 1968.

Lairdscrest, Burns & Laird Line, 1936, 789grt, 72m x 11m, 13½ knots. She was renamed *San Marco* in 1968, *Kronos* in 1975 and broken up in 1978.

Vasilia (1955/979grt) was built for Coast Lines as the *Ulster Premier*, becoming *Kelvin* in 1963 and *Vasilia* in 1968. Renamed *Alftan* in 1972, *Tacamar II* in 1977, *Canaima* in 1982, she was finally broken up in 1983.

Pointer, Coast Lines, 1956, 1,208grt, 68m x 11m, 11½ knots. She was built as *Birchfield* and became *Pointer* in 1959, *Taurus III* in 1975, *Larnaca Town* in 1984, *Mina* in 1985 and was broken up at Perama in 1986.

Inniscarra, B&I Line, 1948, 584grt, 54m x 9m, 11 knots. She was built as *Brittany Coast* and was renamed *Inniscarra* in 1950, *Elni* in 1970, *Ria* in 1972 before being broken up in Italy in 1981.

Opposite: Cheshire Coast (1954/1,202grt), *Inniscarra* (1948/584grt), *Kentish Coast* (1946/498grt) and *Wirral Coast* (1962/881grt) loading cargo in Trafalgar Dock, Liverpool.

Meath, B&I Line, 1960, 1,558grt, 88m x 14m, 13 knots. She was sold to the Vickers Shipbuilding Co. in 1973 and was renamed *Vickers Viscount* in 1975, *British Viscount* in 1980 and *British* in 1990, being broken up at Alang that year.

Hadrian Coast, Coast Lines, 1942, 692grt, 64m x 10m, 11½ knots. She was built as *Empire Atoll* and became *Hadrian Coast* in 1946 and *Elda* in 1967. On 10 January 1970 she grounded off Morocco and was declared a total loss.

Stability, F.T. Everard & Sons, 1949, 1,490grt, 74m x 11m, 11 knots. Renamed *Kingon* and *Projogo I* in 1973 and *Vandara Tana* in 1978, she was broken up in Indonesia in 1986.

Alignity, F.T. Everard & Sons, 1945, 890grt, 61m x 10m, 9½ knots. She was built as *Empire Fitzroy* and was renamed *Alignity* in 1952, being broken up at Blyth where she arrived on 16 November 1971.

Cabourne, Coastal Carriers Ltd, 1931, 528grt, 50m x 8m, 9 knots. Built as *Ngatira*, she became *Springwood* in 1946 and *Cabourne* in 1947.

The Lady Grania (1952/1,152grt) and *Lady Gwendolen* (1953/1,164grt) were owned by Arthur Guinness Son & Co. and traded between Dublin and Liverpool. They are shown here unloading at Salthouse Dock, Liverpool. *The Lady Grania* became *The Lady Scotia* in 1978 and was lost off the Baja peninsular in 1981. *Lady Gwendolen* sank in 1979 following a collision.

British & Continental Steamship Co. vessel *Dotterel*. The line operated services from Liverpool to Rotterdam, Amsterdam, Dunkirk, Antwerp and Ghent. They also operated from Ellesmere Port, Runcorn and Garston to Continental ports.

Oarsman, Rowbotham & Co., 1959, 778grt, 62m x 9m, 10½ knots. She was sold to Normandie Dredging at Southampton in 1974 and renamed *Solent Lee*, being sold again in 1976 to Redland Purle Ltd, Lee Shipping at Hull in 1979 and Solent Aggregates in 1981.

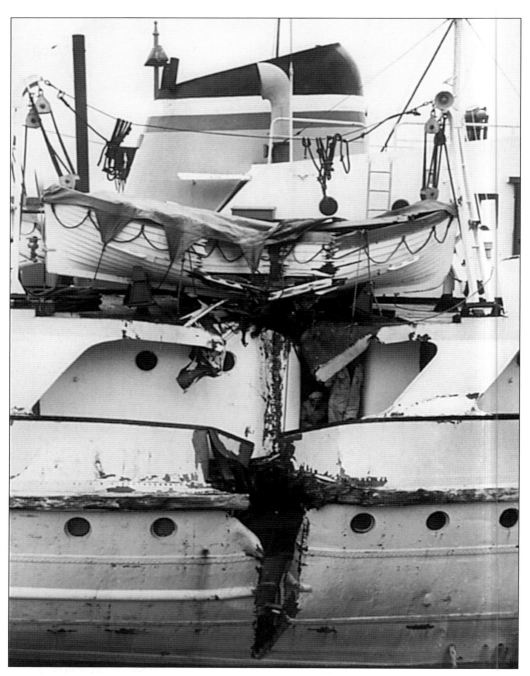

Blackthorn (1960/749grt) arrives at Waterloo Dock following a collision with the United States Lines' vessel *American Veteran* on 10 November 1964. *Blackthorn*, which was bound from Coleraine to pick up a cargo at Garston, was at anchor in the Queens Channel when the accident occurred in thick fog. While *Blackthorn* sustained a 10ft hole in her side, a smashed lifeboat and badly damaged superstructure aft of the bridge, the *American Veteran* was only slightly damaged and none of the crew on either ship were hurt.

Four
Mersey Ferries, Tugs and Dredgers

The Mersey ferries can be traced back to a service provided by Benedictine monks in 1150 and in 1330 King Edward III granted a licence to operate a ferry across the river. Over the centuries ownership of the ferry service changed regularly and, in 1822, a steam-driven ferry was provided on the route along with the introduction of a wooden paddle steamer. The Woodside, Eastham, Egremont, Seacombe and New Brighton services came under the control of local government boards and remained under Birkenhead and Wallasey Corporation control until the services were given to the Merseyside Passenger Transport Authority following the 1968 Transport Act and local government reorganisation in 1974.

The Mersey tugs play a vital role in the efficient operation of the Port of Liverpool. The Alexandra Towing Co., one of the largest tug owners in the UK, was established in 1887 and during the 1960s operated a fleet of forty tugs at Liverpool, Southampton, Swansea and Port Talbot. The company acquired the fleet of the Liverpool Screw Towing Co. in 1966 and the fleet of J.H. Lamey, which operated two of the most powerful diesel tugs on the Mersey, in 1968.

The Rea Towing Co. operated a fleet of thirteen tugs which ranged from 1,200hp to 4,000hp and were fitted with the latest firefighting, salvage and deep sea towing equipment. The company developed from a bunkering service in 1879, and in 1922 the Rea Towing Co. was formed to develop towing services on the Mersey.

Dredging of the docks and channels from the Bar was carried out by specialised dredging vessels owned by the Mersey Docks & Harbour Board and those of the Westminster Dredging Co.

Seacombe ferry *Royal Daffodil* sailed on the Mersey until 1976 when she was sold to operate in Greek w aters.

Royal Iris, Wallasey Corporation, 1951, 1,234grt, 49m x 15m, 12 knots. Sold in 1994, she moved to Cardiff in 1995 and to London in 1998.

Lamey tug *B.C. Lamey* (1966/215grt) became *Salthouse* in 1970, *David F* in 1985 and *Zamtug II* in 1987.

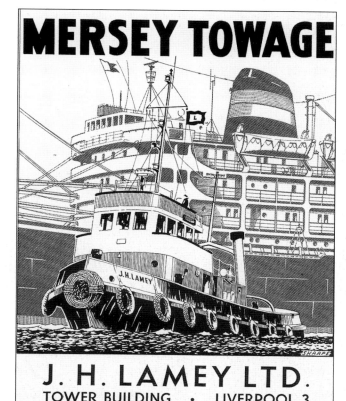

MERSEY TOWAGE

J. H. LAMEY LTD.

TOWER BUILDING · LIVERPOOL 3

TELEPHONE: CENtral 6411-2   TELEGRAMS: "LAMEY-L'POOL 3"

Opposite: Birkenhead Corporation ferry *Overchurch* (1962/468grt) leaves Liverpool Landing Stage in rough weather in 1964.

Above: Aysgarth, Rea Towing Co., 1950, 231grt. She was broken up in 1972 at Troon.

Below: Grassgarth, Rea Towing Co., 1953, 231grt. She was broken up at Troon in 1972.

Applegarth, Rea Towing Co., 1951, 231grt. She was sold and renamed *Afon Cefni* in 1971, *Achilles* in 1973 and *Vernicos Christina* in 1975. She was broken up at Perama in 1980.

Throstlegarth, Rea Towing Co., 1954, 231grt. Sold to the West of Scotland Shipbreaking Co., she arrived at Troon on 11 November 1972 for breaking up.

Trafalgar, Alexandra Towing Co., 1966, 174grt. Sold in 1992 and renamed *Megalochari VII*, she was sold by Proodos Naftiki, Eteria, Greece, to Agia Marina N.E., Greece, in 2000 and was renamed *Agia Marina*.

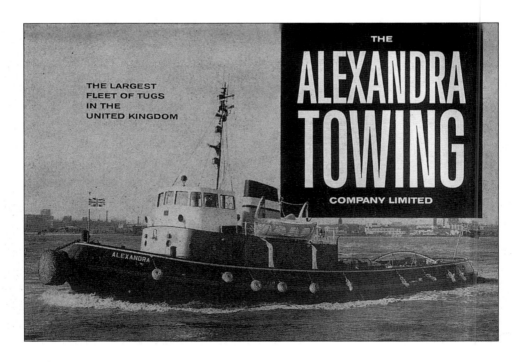

Nelson, Alexandra Towing Co., 1966, 175grt. She sank in the River Mersey off Garston in 1995 and was broken up.

Canada, Alexandra Towing Co., 1951, 237grt. Renamed *Strepitoso* in 1969, she was broken up at Brindisi where demolition commenced on 21 December 1988.

LIVERPOOL SCREW TOWING COMPANY

Above: Fighting Cock, Liverpool Screw Towing Co., 1953, 218grt. She was renamed *Sloyne* in 1971 and *Vernicos Nicos* in 1972.

Below: West Cock, Liverpool Screw Towing Co., 1958, 193grt. Renamed *Morpeth* in 1970 and *Vernicos Giannis* in 1981, she sank off Iraklion, Greece in 1983. She was refloated but later lost off Falconera.

Services offered to shipping operators on Merseyside in 1964.

Norwest, Norwest Sand & Gravel Co., 1955, 596grt, 46m x 11m, 9½ knots. She became *Couesnom* in 1989.

Hemsley I, Hemsley Bell Ltd, 1916. She was built as *Scotol*, becoming *Hemsley I* in 1947. On 12 May 1969 she ran aground at Fox's Cove near Padstow and was demolished.

Arnet Robinson, Mersey Docks & Harbour Board, 1958, 734grt, 54m x 10m, 12 knots. In 1982 she was converted from a pilot boat to a hydrographic and seismographic research ship, renamed *Pensurveyor*. In 1988 she was bought by Turkish owners, converted to a ferry and renamed *Faith*.

Mersey No.26, Mersey Docks & Harbour Board, 1948, 1,363grt, 73m x 12m, 11 knots. Renamed *Triaena* in 1974 and broken up at Gijon where she arrived on 19 February that year in tow from Liverpool.

Mersey Compass, Mersey Docks & Harbour Board, 1961, 2,083grt, 84m x 15m, 11 knots. She was sold in 1982 to Dutch owners and retained her name.

W.D. Fairway, Westminster Dredging Co., 1941, 1,299grt, 69m x 12m, 11 knots. She was built as *Theda* and broken up at Runcorn in 1977.